David Anders...

Christmas, 1972

from Gar

STOP-ACTION

STOP-ACTION

DICK BUTKUS

AND ROBERT W. BILLINGS

E. P. DUTTON & CO., INC. | NEW YORK | 1972

STOP-ACTION

1

Saturday, December 11

Eight o'clock in the morning and this kid is jumping on my chest. Four years old, but when you're asleep he hits like Csonka, and I sure don't get a kick out of it. That'll teach me to make promises. I'm learning a lesson from my own kid. Never make a promise if you don't intend to keep it, or you'll regret it.

Rick wanted to play football last night but it was already past his bedtime so I told him to wait till today.

Okay, wait till I get up. Get the ball. Stand over there. That's a boy. Okay, throw the ball. All right, now catch it. Keep your elbows in. Okay, now run. I'll get you.

He catches the ball and gets down in one of those lopsided kids' stances and runs at me. I get down on the floor and throw pillows at his legs as if a goose-down man was trying to tackle him.

Get up Rick. Get up. Come on. Run. Run. Run. Touchdown!

I often wonder if I laughed like Nikki and Ricky when I was a kid. I suppose all kids do. It's almost hysterical. You think almost any minute they're going to lose complete control and fly.

Time to get dressed and go to the ten o'clock meeting.

Normally when we're going out of town we have a practice at about eight for an hour or so. Then we're on our own until we assemble at the airport at about one. But today we're not flying up to Green Bay until four. They thought we were going to beat Denver last week and that would give us a good shot at the playoffs. And because Detroit and Minnesota were playing at noon today they thought we better leave later so we could all watch the game on television. I don't know why. You can't see that much, and we're going to see the movies later anyway. It was stupid. And then we blew the Denver game anyway. But they still didn't change the itinerary. So now I have to drive about fifty miles round trip just for a damn twenty-minute meeting.

Now just sit back and enjoy the ride. Relax. It's just like the entertainment business. I'm here to perform. If I wasn't here who would be? I'm not only myself but a part of other people's lives.

He was born December 9, 1942, and christened Richard Marvin, the fifth son and seventh child of Emma and John Butkus. With two daughters, Lee and Alberta, and then four sons, John, Ronald, Donald, and David, Mrs. Butkus was hoping for another daughter.

At over thirteen pounds Butkus was the biggest baby born in Roseland that year, but his late arrival brought with it some complications and for four days he fought for life in an incubator.

Emma Goodoff's parents came from Lithuania and settled in the coal town of Ladd, Illinois, where her father worked in the mines. When the mines played out the family moved to Rockford, Illinois.

John Butkus emigrated to Canada from Lithuania just before the first world war. He boomed his way through the logging and mining camps of central Canada and picked up the electrician's trade before he made his way down to the southeast side of Chicago, the Roseland area, about fourteen miles south of the Loop.

Emma and John met at a picnic one summer when she was in Chicago visiting a sister. A few years after that they purchased a modest bungalow at 10324 South Lowe Avenue. It remained the family home for almost forty-five years.

Everyone in the Butkus family is big. Only John, the eldest brother, is smaller than Dick. They are all fine athletes. The nickel-dime poker games at their mother's house are still an almost weekly feature of their lives.

As a young boy Dick didn't seem to be fulfilling the

8

promise of his thirteen-pound, record-setting birth. For a long time he was the smallest kid in the neighborhood. He served as the water boy for his brothers' team and hauled their equipment to Fernwood Park in his coaster wagon.

His first game was baseball. He loved it and was good at it. It made his mother hope that there would be some future in it for him, a game removed from that brutal football which her other sons all played. "I vowed that he would never be a football player," Mrs. Butkus said. "My other sons played it and I didn't want to see him getting hurt."

I never thought about playing pro ball. I just wanted to keep playing and so kept moving up from one level to the next. There were so many times that something could have screwed me up. How many guys know what they want to do when they are six or seven—and do it? I did. I wanted to play football. I was able to do things on the field that others couldn't. It gave people enjoyment, satisfied them in some way. That's why I listened to that guy Foudini.

He came to some of the practices early in the year. He was talking to Jack Concannon and Brupbacher. He told Bru he had a vision of what was going to happen this year. So Bru started to tell some of the guys about it. I didn't pay much attention. Then right at the beginning of the season Bru came in and wanted everybody to sign a ball. He said it was for Foudini. Foudini told Concannon and Abe Gibron that Jack had to shave off his sideburns and moustache or else he was going to get hurt in the L.A. game. We all thought we could beat L.A. especially after winning our first two. So we go out there and lost and wouldn't you know it Concannon hurt his knee and had to have an operation the next day.

Everybody quit laughing about Foudini. One day Bru came in and told me that Foudini wanted to talk to me about a diet.

Foudini's a little guy in his middle to late forties. He was wearing those workman's wash pants and a zipper jacket. He said he worked in a steel mill about two hundred miles from Chicago. He started right in telling me he could have helped the Cubs if they would have let him talk to the players. Then he went on to the Frisco game coming up the next weekend. "You guys are going to be in the lead all the way and you're going to run into a little trouble." He said if Kent Nix has some difficulty in the first half tell him to put on some white shoes because white is true and it signified holiness and that's how God is. I asked him, "Well, what if Doug and me wear white shoes?" He said it doesn't matter with you guys as long as the quarterback wears the white shoes. I went along with him. I don't know why. He told me that he could only communicate with me, Brupbacher, and Concannon to get his feelings back to the players because we are Catholics. Then he told me to tell Cecil Turner to wear white shoes because he was hesitating on the punt and kickoff returns. Nix changed his shoes and we did everything else Foudini wanted but we still lost 13–0. The offense just couldn't capitalize on anything.

But the whole thing is funny. You know when you're winning you'd do almost anything to keep that streak going. After we lost, I said the hell with it. If we're going to lose, we're going to lose. If I'm going to get hurt, I'm going to get hurt. I'm funny that way. I believe in people visualizing what's going to happen. It's kind of far-fetched but the same thing happens to me on the field. People say, he's got a knack for the ball. It's just that I've been there before and done it before. It's almost as if I have a vision that I know what's going to happen. Perhaps it's just instinct. Anyway, that's what leads me to be a little superstitious.

I can remember lying on the floor when I was a kid and watching the College All-Star game. "I'll be playing in that some day," I told my parents. I don't remember exactly what my mother said, but it was as if she knew it too. Really knew it not just saying it. It's weird. There were so many things that could have happened to sidetrack me or wash me out of football. I don't know if everyone is predestined or not but everything I did, all my work, was pointed in the direction of football. I only took jobs that would help build me up for football. Maybe it wasn't destiny but I like to think it was—and if it was I really can't take much credit for it, can I?

All we did in the meeting was watch a kicking reel of Green Bay and Abe Gibron, one of our defensive coaches, talked about a few things we had to do to stop the Packers' running game.

The safeties, Jerry Moore and Ron Smith, and the cornerbacks, Joe Taylor and Charlie Ford, have to read the run a little quicker and come up faster to keep them from turning the corner. Once you let anybody turn that corner you're in trouble. The first time we played them we were letting them get around too easy. That's what I had to drive an hour and a half to listen to, and then drive all the way home and then later all the way back to the airport.

On the way home I had to stop by and pick up Helen's mother, Mrs. Helen Essenberg, who still lives in the old neighborhood around 113th Street and Wentworth. Helen is driving up to Green Bay for the game with some friends. She'll be leaving before I do, so her mother is going to baby-sit over the weekend. My ma and dad either go to the game or watch it on television, but Helen's mother doesn't really care for sports so she watches the kids.

The first thing I saw when I got back on the expressway were these great clouds of brownish-black smoke spewing out from the big stacks at the Sherwin-Williams paint company at 115th Street. Great clouds of pollution and it stunk. It smelled like fried paint. We started to talk about it and I said, "They ought to investigate that place. When the wind is from the west it blows out across Lake Calumet, but when the wind is from the east or northeast it pollutes the entire southeast side of the city."

I was born and raised in that neighborhood, but now I wonder why anyone would want to live there. If I had my way I'd spend my time in either Florida or Colorado, somewhere out West. You've got room to breathe. The air is clear. You can even see the stars at night.

I slipped downstairs for a little nap before lunch but Nikki and Ricky were down there building with their blocks. I was no sooner lying down than Ricky came at me with one of his flying leaps. We started wrestling around and fighting and then Nikki rushed in to help.

When the call for lunch finally came I went upstairs and turned on the television set so I could watch the Detroit-Minnesota game while I ate. Nikki put on the set in the kitchen for herself. She was paying more attention to Batman than to her food so I snatched her hamburger when her back was turned.

When she turned back to pick up more potato chips she looked at her plate and then at me, but I put on an innocent face.

I don't know if I was having more fun fooling around with Nikki or watching the Lions get their asses beaten. I was just waiting for the announcer to start saying something, to start talking about All-World Lucci or Flanagan. They were getting killed, wiped out.

Alan Page had the most outstanding day I've ever seen a defensive lineman have. He literally did it all by himself. In a two-minute sequence near the end of the first half he was in on eight or nine straight plays; dumping Landry, or making the tackle at the line if they ran at him, or pursuing and making the tackle if they tried to go away from him, or having the offensive guard called for holding him. He also blocked a kick. I don't think I've ever seen one man make so many outstanding plays, and especially not one right on top of another the way he did it to the Lions.

I was fascinated watching Page. He doesn't wear any tape on his hands. Maybe he'll tape a couple of fingers together if they're a little sprained. He doesn't wear any forearm pads or elbow pads. He doesn't need them. It's because he's so quick. He never really makes contact with anybody on the line. He doesn't hit anybody. He's so quick he's by the blocker before the guy can make contact. He's right around him.

If there's anybody who should be Defensive Player of the Year it's him. He was behind me in the voting last year, but this year I think he'll get it. He scores more himself, a defensive tackle, than a lot of running backs. He's scored a couple of safeties, blocked a couple of punts and a field goal or two. He's truly a great player. I think he could play just about anywhere you asked him to and do a helluva job.

Helen left with our friends Joe Elias and his wife, Jan, and then it was time for me to get ready. The kids started fighting about something. Ricky took one of Nikki's smile stickers and pasted it on her fish bowl. She was crying and yelling and he was teasing her. My mother-in-law couldn't control them. It seems that nothing means anything to them unless I say it.

I called Nikki into the bedroom and she told me what was wrong. Then I used my Florida threat. "You better behave if you want to go to Florida." I'm leaving right after the last game. I can't wait to get out of here, but they don't know that. All they know is no swimming, no fishing if you don't behave. So far its been working pretty well.

I picked up the end of the game on the car radio. With about a minute or two to go Cuozzo tried a couple of long bombs. The announcer said, "Well, it looks like Grant's sure trying to pour it on. You know these guys will have their day too. These things have a way of evening themselves out. They'll get theirs too."

When I heard the guy talking like that I naturally assumed it was a Detroit station. It figures. It kind of fits in with the Detroit team. I think they are a lot of jerks, from the owner, the general manager, the coach on down. Even the announcers must be a bunch of fags. If we were voting for a jerk team or organization they'd have my vote all the way.

I passed some kids playing touch football in a school yard. What fun that used to be. No pressure. No big deal. Play quarterback, or be a receiver and run out for passes. I thought about those games in the school yard and in Fernwood Park with Rick Richards and Rick Bertetto and Bob Rittmeyer and all the old gang. After we'd get through we'd go over and sneak in Gately Stadium and watch some of the high school games. Then on the way home we'd grab someone's hat and use it for a ball. We'd play on everyone's front lawn all the way home. We'd form a line and the guy with the hat would try to run through everyone. Running or tackling, I enjoyed them both.

Sometimes I'd have to sort of force the other guys to play. Sometimes we'd go back to the park, get a ball, and start playing all over again. How can anyone ever get enough?

At home after I watched a game on television I'd go into the bedroom, or sometimes late at night when everyone else was asleep, I'd roll a pair of socks into a ball and I'd throw it up like it was a kickoff. I'd catch it and run along the bed on my knees, and I'd go down as if I were tackled, or I'd lunge into the pillows as if I were trying to make a first down.

It really didn't feel like I was on my way to a game today. For one thing we were leaving at four instead of about one. And for another we're out of it, out of the playoffs. The only thing I had on my mind was leaving for Florida. That's all that's been on my mind for the past several weeks now. I use it to threaten the kids, but if they only knew how anxious I was to leave they'd laugh at me. If the club weren't having a day and a party for Ed O'Bradovich right after the game I think I'd leave then to get it all behind me as soon as possible.

This is the last road game, I said to myself walking to the plane, the last time this year that we'll be able to play Boo-Ray. That's a card game we play to pass the time on the Saturday flights. Once we're on the plane everybody breaks down into their own little groups. Ours is usually Jim Cadile, Randy Jackson, Fig Newton, Doug Buffone, O'B, and sometimes Ross Brupbacher. We're the Boo-Ray gang.

Don't ask me what the game means or where it came from or who started it. They were playing it on the Bears long before I got here and they play it on all the other teams around the league. It's simple to play. Deal everyone five cards and then turn one over for trumps.

From the dealer's left you go in order and declare whether you're going to stay or drop out. If you stay you have to take at least one trick. If you stay and don't take a trick you've just been Boo-Rayed. Then you have to match the pot. You're a cinch if you have the ace of trumps, but sometimes it can get a little tricky. You might have three low trumps and still not take a trick.

The bidding can be more fun than the playing sometimes. Everyone seems to have his own favorite way of saying he's dropping out of the hand. A plain old pass is never good enough. Listening to these guys I get the idea I'm either watching or I'm in a TV Western. O'Bradovich's favorite is "I fold like a sad sack of shit." Jackson always says "foldolo." No two guys will use the same expression.

If they're going to play they never just say so. It's always I'll dance, or I'll skate, and Ed'll say, I'll waltz. It's not hard to tell when Ed is loaded. It shows all over his big face. If everyone passes, the dealer takes the pot.

On the flight to Denver the week before I set a record by winning $85. Since this was a short flight, only forty minutes or so, no one was going to have time to threaten that. Buffone was threatening another record, the one for a loser set by Ralph Kurek a couple of years ago when he lost $34 on one flight.

Since it was such a short flight, and since it was the last flight of the year, we decided to play the last game for $5 a man instead of the usual $1. Everyone passed but Doug and O'B. And O'B Boo-Rayed him. We thought Buffone had tied the old mark for a loser and we were all laughing about it and stood up to give Doug a hand when Bru started shouting, "Wait a minute! Wait a minute!"

Bru was the scorekeeper and he had rechecked the score sheet and found that Doug had only lost $33 instead of $35, so Kurek's old record of $34 still stood. Everybody in the plane started booing Doug and jeering him.

"You're all nothing but fans," Doug hollered back.

On the way down we were arguing and trying to decide who we'd send as our representatives if we could arrange a Boo-Ray Pro Bowl, two players from each team, single elimination, the games to be played on a flight from New York to L.A. Everyone, naturally, thought they ought to be one of the team. The plane landed before we got that straightened out.

It was dark in Green Bay and there was snow on the ground. Ed said he couldn't wait until it snowed so he could go snow-mobiling. He said after the last game he was going to do nothing but go snowmobiling with his kid for two weeks. "Maybe you're going to go snowmobiling," I told him, "but I'm going to play in the warm water on the beach in Florida. I just don't like this cold anymore."

Went all the way to the back of the bus and just tried to get as comfortable as possible.

It doesn't even seem like a game anymore. When you've been around for a few years you know there's nothing you can do if you're out of it. You just have to play for yourself. For your own pride and self-respect. That's hard to do because it doesn't look like we're ever going anywhere. It'd be different if we were improving, but we're on the skids. We, the defense, are going to be on that field a long time tomorrow. Between their running game and our running game our offense can't do anything—one touchdown in four games.

15

The Northland Hotel is usually crowded. It's the headquarters for everyone who comes up from Chicago and from all over Wisconsin for the Bears-Packers games. Besides, it's about the only hotel in town. Everyone knows we stay there and the lobby is always full of autograph hounds. But today there was no one there. The place was empty. Even at the airport there's usually such a big crowd on hand that we jump on the buses out on the runway. But today we just walked right through the terminal building. It was kind of a relief, and at the same time kind of a disappointment. We began kidding ourselves about the advantages of losing—no mob of people crowding around, pawing at you, bugging you for autographs. Winners get the crowds. Losers they leave alone.

It's a real old hotel, and we got up to the room and took one look around at the two, little, sagging three-by-six beds and Ed walked over to the little TV set in the corner, switched it on, and all the time he was muttering, "First class, first class all the way."

We sat in that dark, dingy, gloomy room and watched the end of the Miami-Baltimore game. We started bitching and comparing their organizations to ours. Here's Miami, a fairly new team, an expansion team, leading their division. And we talked about the Baltimore organization and Ed was talking about the way they conduct their practices compared to ours and I was just shaking my head and he was rambling on and on.

We'd probably still be going if it wasn't for the team meeting. We had one scheduled for six. I think they do that just to make sure no one is running around town. But where would you go in Green Bay, Wisconsin? L.A., Miami, Frisco, or New York maybe, but there's no place to go in Green Bay.

We were heading for the same room we've had our meeting in once a year for as long as I've been with the Bears. And for some reason or other I remembered the first meeting I ever went to in that room. It was my rookie year, 1965, and the Old Man, George Halas senior himself, was still coaching. Hell he was only sixty-nine or seventy then. We had lost our first two games that year out on the Coast and here we were in Green Bay to play the Packers, and that's when the Packers were really the Packers.

Things didn't look too good for our side. We were zero and two going in and just about everybody figured we would be zero and three coming out. To get us in the proper frame of mind the Old Man started telling us a story about Lord Baltimore. He was telling us about some battle where the underdogs were taking their usual beating and then along galloped Lord Baltimore. He came on and led the rag-tag army to victory even though all the odds were stacked against him. We really couldn't understand what the hell he was talking about and what that had to do with Jimmy Taylor and Bart Starr, and we kept sneaking looks at each other and shrugging our shoulders and raising our eyebrows.

The Old Man finished up by saying, "That's what this team needs. We need someone like Lord Baltimore to pull us through tomorrow, because gentlemen, we are certainly underdogs. But we could pull through if we could find a leader out on that field, someone like Lord Baltimore."

When he finished we broke down into our separate offensive and defensive team meetings. The offense always stays right where they are. It's always the defense that gets chased down the hall somewhere. As we were going to our meeting room we had to walk out on a balcony that overlooks the main lobby. There was a big wedding reception going on, and I'll never forget it, as we're walking out on that balcony Doug Atkins starts yelling out,

"Paging Lord Baltimore! Paging Lord Baltimore! Lord Baltimore we need you! Help us Lord Baltimore wherever you are!"

We all started cracking up and roaring and all the people in the lobby looked up and either started laughing with us or thought we were crazy. It was impossible for the Old Man not to have heard it. I kept waiting for a bolt of lightning or something to strike Atkins. After all, George Halas practically invented pro football.

This afternoon Abe just went over a few things. What more was there to say anyway. He said we'd go over everything again tomorrow anyway so take off and take it easy. Willie Holman was smiling and Abe asked him what the hell was so funny, meaning that tomorrow was going to be a tough game on us and he didn't know what the hell we were laughing at. So we all started laughing and then tough old Abe cracked a little himself.

A short meeting meant I had time on my hands. Helen called earlier and I had a date to meet her for dinner about seven. I don't know why I told her to come by so late, so I went down to the lobby with Spot and talked with him for a while. Spot is Jerry Moore, our rookie safety man. We named him Spot after the dog with the big, black eye patch in Spanky and the Little Rascals because in the twelve games we've played he must have had a black eye on one side or the other every single week.

A couple of people asked for autographs and then this woman, I can't really call her a lady, came over and said she wanted our autographs. She must have been about forty or so, one of those bottle blonds, and drunk.

"I don't know who you are, but I want your autographs."

She was swaying a little from side to side. I just sat there for a few minutes looking at her and Spot was looking at me and shaking his head at that drunken broad and she kept it up.

"I don't have any paper or pencil, but I want your autographs, even though I don't know who you are."

I got up and walked away and Moore started laughing. He must have thought I was going for paper and pencil. I just can't understand people, how they can go out of their way to make asses of themselves. And they think they're clever or cute while they're doing it. It really disgusts me.

Helen and I went to a place named McCall's with my brothers, Don and John, and their wives, and friends of John's, Russ and Barbara Scaramella, and Joe Elias and Jan. We had a good meal. I had a lobster and half of Helen's prime rib.

While we were eating there were the usual annoyances. A couple of guys came by and slapped me on the back and said something like "we've come a long way. You better win tomorrow."

Then some Packer fan came by while I was eating and started pawing me and he said, "You know Dick, I hope you do well, but I hope your team loses."

It gets ridiculous sometimes. I suppose the ones who are doing it don't think so, but I think it's damn ignorant. What the hell, I don't go to a restaurant to entertain anybody. I go there to eat.

And I'm not there to sign autographs. Starting at about noon to-morrow, that's when my act starts. That's when I belong to the public.

Despite the interruptions we managed to have some fun—a lot of laughs and kidding around. I was teasing John about his son Jimmy, my nephew. He won a scholarship to Illinois. He's very good in math and he wants to major in physics. John is very proud of him. You can hear it in his voice. He was asking me if I knew some people down there who could get him a job because even with the scholarship he'd have some expenses.

And I said, "Go on, the kid is nothing but a bookworm. I don't want to be embarrassed by having people think I associate with bookworms."

John said he was a good kid and wasn't a bookworm. He's interested in sports and books and that wouldn't hurt any of us.

But I wouldn't let him off too easy. "Not only is he a bookworm, but also he's the kind of guy who'd squeal on struggling athletes trying to cheat their way through an exam."

We kept it up for a while and then I thought I better lay off before John wrapped his sirloin around my neck so I changed the subject to Florida and the great fishing down there. I'd like my folks to come down and stay with us. They say, yes, they'd like to go, but that's as far as it ever gets with them.

Anyway, that's how we spend Saturday night in the big leagues. I got back to that wonderful room of ours and Ed wasn't in yet so I turned on some old movie and started reviewing the game plan. I must have dozed off. He came in slamming things around, like he usually does, and woke me up.

He and Bru had gone over to the Left Guard, Fuzzy Thurston's place. He told me it was jammed as usual. That got us talking about all those guys who played under Lombardi in those winning years and how well they all seemed to be doing. Fuzzy's got six or eight restaurants throughout Wisconsin and he's gotta be making nothing but money. He's really a great guy. Couldn't be a nicer guy, and he was a helluva player. And we talked about Kramer and Hornung and Taylor and all those guys and Starr and Willie Davis, who's now with the Schlitz brewery.

19

I turned off the lights and waited for Abe to come by and tuck me in.

"Butkus!"

"Yeah."

"Okay."

2

Sunday, December 12

Nitschke Day. Today the Packers fans are honoring Ray Nitschke, the man who helped them win so many championships back in the glory days.

How lucky he was to play for a man like Lombardi. All those great years they had, and I remember Fuzzy telling me, you would have really loved to play for Lombardi. And I was thinking, wondering what would have happened if somehow I started out in Green Bay. You know how when your mind wanders you can almost see things clearly, the images of people and situations, almost as clearly as real life.

Where I would have played. Lombardi didn't like to play rookies, and Ray was in his prime. Would I have been content to play on the special teams and sit on the bench, but still be with a winner? Be satisfied getting all that extra money? Or should I be content doing what I did with the Bears?

I remembered how I used to watch Ray. I've always said I've never had an idol, even when I was a kid. I just kept my eyes on my own level, but I suppose the one player I admired most was Ray Nitschke.

I met him for the first time when I was in college, a sophomore at Illinois. Ray had gone to Illinois a few years before, and he was down there for a visit of some kind. We were introduced and he seemed friendly. We made some small talk. I don't remember what it was. Nothing important. Probably something like keep your head up, or wash behind your ears at night.

I'm sure I didn't say much, because I never do in those situations. And, I was probably feeling a little self-conscious. But that's not important. He made me feel that here was a big man, a man already doing and being what I wanted to do and be, and he was good enough to take the time to talk to me.

A month or so later the Packers were in the championship game against the Giants. I can still remember sitting in front of the television set trying to help Ray make every tackle. It gave me a great thrill when they made the post-game announcement that he had been named the game's most valuable player. If he asked me I would have gladly served as the chauffeur for the sports car they gave him.

Two years later we were both on the same field playing in the annual Bears-Packers charity exhibition game in Milwaukee. After the game we met in the middle of the field and shook hands. We talked for a while, just the how ya doin' kind of stuff, and finally we both turned and went our separate ways. We really haven't had much to say to each other since.

Twelve thirteen: Mac Percival, our place-kicker, comes by and says, "let's go," and the early birds hit the field. It's something to do besides sitting around the locker room and nervously walking to the toilet every five minutes. Howard Mudd would be so worked up before the games that he'd get to the locker room about eight o'clock and keep throwing up right up till the kickoff.

You can get too tensed up just sitting around, so when Mac the Foot goes out to hit some kickoffs and field goals we go shag the balls for him. I started when I was a rookie back in 1965. There are about seven or eight of us ball shaggers and we try to keep it strictly for defensive players.

It's a relaxed and easy time. The fans yell things down at us, and we holler back at them. It's a nice day to be outside, clear and sunny, in the thirty's, and the field is just a bit soft. The fans start in on me right away.

"Hey Butkus, get a haircut. Hey Butkus, did you bring your Rise? Hey Butkus, you'll get yours"—friendly things like that.

Sometimes I holler back. A couple of years ago when we were still playing our home games in Wrigley Field a fan sitting in the end zone tried to keep a ball that Mac had boomed into the seats. He wouldn't throw it back and I yelled up at him and called him a name. Don Shinnick was going by then and he stopped, shook his head, and said, "Uh-uh, uh-uh, shouldn't be talking like that. Those are paying customers." Shinnick is one of those Fellowship of Christian Athletes guys. Never swears. The worst thing I've ever heard him say is, "What the rip!"

He's a funny guy. This is his second year as coach of the linebackers. He was a great linebacker with the Colts for years and years. There are all kinds of stories about him when he was a player, that he was some kind of flake. He likes to wear white shoes. Wears them in any kind of weather. Last year in New Orleans for our final game of the season he had the entire defensive team in white shoes. He said he was going to try and get us shoes made in our team colors, orange and blue.

During the warm-up sessions he keeps walking by and asking out of the corner of his mouth—"think anybody's watching? Think they notice my white shoes?" It sounds a little silly maybe, but he does it just to keep us loose.

We line up for calisthenics and I know it's time for Abe Gibron to come around. Abe is our other defensive coach. He's gruff and straight talking. He really doesn't talk. He growls. Abe is short and bald and about as wide as he is high. He weighs about three hundred, give or take thirty to forty pounds, and he's always on a new diet.

In his days with the Cleveland Browns and the Bears he was one of the best and fastest offensive guards in the game. They tell the story that whenever Paul Brown wanted to cut an interior lineman he'd tell the guy it was down to him and Abe and whomever would win a forty-yard dash would make the team. Nobody could beat Abe despite his five-by-five appearance and Brown knew it.

Abe is from the old school and believes in all the manly virtues, like never wearing a warm-up jacket, even if it's ten below. He says warm-up jackets are okay for offensive players because they're just touch-tackle players anyway. But defensive players have to be tough, so we don't wear them. We could never really be rough and tough enough for Abe. He's a very excitable type and quite a contrast from Shinnick. In the heat of the game he might tear off his cap and stomp on it and holler at the players, but in a crisis he thinks clearly. Abe is always prowling around, always behind me during the drills, always telling me, "Keep 'em up. Keep 'em going. Don't let them get down. No matter what happens early, keep 'em going. Keep 'em going and we'll always be in the game."

Shinnick is quieter. After every game he comes up to each defensive player and asks how he feels. Sometimes Abe does it but Shinnick does it all the time. It makes you feel good to know that a coach takes an interest in you as something other than just a body to plug up a hole.

The Packers were late taking the field. They didn't come out until we were already doing our calisthenics. They were all wearing warm-up jackets. Everyone that is except number sixty-six, Ray Nitschke. I just had to laugh a little when I thought how pleased Abe would be with Nitschke. We went back in to put on the pads.

This is when the tension usually begins. I try to concentrate on the simplest of jobs, like taping my hands or putting on a dry T-shirt. I focus on the little adjustments to make sure the tape is just right, not too loose and not so tight that it cuts off the circulation. But today, nothing. It didn't even feel like a game. It was like, well, we're here, so we might as well go through with it. There's nothing to prove. Just go out and put on a good show. I'm so damn tired of losing.

You work so damn hard to get here. All your life you work hard to get to play in the pros and then the end of the season comes, the time when there should be some rewards and instead you end up with a season like ours and all you want to do is go off and hide somewhere.

I tried to get my mind to work for me. I tried to get myself up. I thought about everything I did to get here. I went to camp with the rookies this year. If you've never been to Rensselaer, Indiana, in July, you've got a treat coming. The sun seems to hang straight up all day. By ten you're choking on dust and gasping on humidity. Instead of water you get to watch the heat waves floating over the corn fields. I could barely run. But I had something to run for. I had to prove it all over again. The past is gone, I kept telling myself. You have to prove it all over again.

A few weeks before camp I saw a magazine story that said that with Butkus hobbled with a surgical knee this was going to be the year Mike Curtis finally gets the recognition he deserves as the best middle linebacker in football. When I saw that story I sat down and had a long talk with my knee. I told my knee all about it. All during camp, whenever I felt like taking it easy, I'd remind my knee of Curtis and that story. C'mon knee, just a little bit more for Mike Curtis.

In the past I was always able to find something I could use as a spur, as a whip against myself. When I was in high school we used to put a car in the middle of a dead-end street and push it back and forth, up and down the street.

I'd spend hours pushing that car trying to build up my legs. I always wanted to push it further, faster, and longer than anyone else. I'd imagine I'd be pushing entire teams up and down the field. In college, and in my first couple of years with the Bears, I didn't know how hard I had to work to accomplish what I wanted. Just as I was learning, along came my knee. That gave me something to push for again, to be able to come back. But today something's missing.

We go over to the blackboard and Abe and Shinnick are going over the things we have to do. Abe is talking about their runs and traps and how Brockington gets to the hole real fast, and how the safeties and cornerbacks have to read the run quickly to keep them from turning the corner.

I wasn't really paying too much attention to what Abe was saying. In the game films I saw what I had been doing wrong that first game when Brockington had such a big day against us. I wasn't taking the blockers on right. I was trying to fight them off with my hands too much. I was too concerned about keeping them away from my legs. I was giving ground and not getting rid of them soon enough. I have to just go right up there and put my shoulder into them and get a stand-off right at the line of scrimmage. If the runner tries to bounce or slide someone else will get him.

I told myself to get ready because with Nitschke on the field and this being his day people are naturally bound to be making comparisons. Besides, with our offense, the way they're going now, you wouldn't have to be a Nitschke to look good. But I knew it wasn't going to be a real emotional day for me. Nobody felt very excited. Usually you see guys tight-lipped with concentration, like their mind is trying to swallow the blackboard. But not today.

Dooley calls us all together. He usually talks so fast that the words and phrases dangle out unconnected and incomplete. His thoughts are way out in front of him. But not today. The word is that the Old Man is going to fire Dooley. Dooley has spent his entire life in the Bears' organization. First as a player, then as an assistant coach, then as defensive coach and as offensive coach and when the Old Man stepped down after forty-nine years as head coach he named Dooley to succeed him.

When we got off to such a great start everyone was talking about Dooley as a coach of the year candidate. Things can change so fast in a couple of weeks. Now he looks and acts like a man who knows his number's up. The offense has scored one touchdown in the last four games. He's the guy who's responsible. He's the guy who has to take the blame.

To tell you the truth I don't even know what he said. He was out of the locker room in a minute. It was so quiet you could hear guys breathing. Every sound was exaggerated. No one said anything. None of the guys were pounding each other on the shoulder pads and chanting, "Let's go, let's go, let's go." That's for winners. We just sat there, everyone thinking his private thoughts.

Sometimes the captains are asked to speak. Whenever I'm called upon I just say something like, "Let's play hard. Let's don't get embarrassed. Let's not have anyone able to point a finger at anyone else and say he didn't give one hundred percent. Let's not any of us come in after the game and say to ourselves, if I would have done this or that things would have been different today."

But I didn't say anything. No one did. We were dead. Finally someone poked his head in the door and said, "Let's go." We got up and quietly walked out for the introductions.

We came out into the tunnel and standing there just back of the opening was Ray Nitschke. He must have come back in after the ceremony they had for him. He was standing there with his back to us as we crowded, almost noiselessly, into the tunnel.

I had an urge, a feeling, to go up to him and stick out my hand and say, "Congratulations Ray, you deserve it." I should have moved toward him as soon as I got the feeling. But I didn't. I'm sorry now I didn't. It's just another one of those things you know you should do, and you know if you don't that you'll always regret it. But before I could make up my mind and get past the guys who were standing between us they were calling out my name and I was running out into the bright sunlight and thundering boos of the Green Bay fans. My kind of people.

After our introduction, and to give Ray one more salute, they also introduced the Green Bay defensive team. Standing there on the sidelines listening I couldn't help remembering how I used to follow his career. He was the one player I most admired. I used to like to watch him, and somehow, for some reason, those Thanksgiving games between the Packers and the Lions stand out in my memory.

Looking around the stadium they had a lot of signs and banners for him. What a great achievement it is to play for fourteen years like he did, and to be on top most of those years. I wondered if anyone would ever have a day like that for me, and how really great Ray must feel today.

Then I contrasted it with what our club is doing for O'Bradovich, or what they're not doing for him next Sunday. The Bears won't even make an announcement at half time that there's a dinner in his honor that night.

All the Packers players were introduced and at the very end it came: ". . . at middle linebacker—number sixty-six—Ray Nitschke." But I don't really think anyone heard anything past the word middle. They were on their feet as he ran out of the tunnel. Fifty thousand people standing and cheering Ray Nitschke.

We kicked off and on the very first play, just a straight drop back pass, Carroll Dale took off. He flew right down the sideline with Joe Taylor on him all alone because we were revolving our zone to the wide side of the field. Joe slipped in the mud and Scott Hunter threw it and they had six points.

That didn't bother or upset me. I just shrugged it off and lined up to try and block the extra point. I felt we were going to do a good job, but I didn't get emotional about it. I figured we could stop their running game if I did my job. Our game plan was to stop their running game and make them throw the ball.

We stayed that way through the first quarter. We stopped their running game, but our offense wasn't moving the ball either. Then in the second quarter we got an interception and Kent Nix threw one to George Farmer for a touchdown. We forced a few more turnovers, but the offense couldn't get it in. Percival missed a couple of field goals, from the twenty-one and the thirty-seven. Normally they'd be easy for Mac, but the guy is really snakebit. He missed some easy ones at Denver last week that cost us the game and now he's really psyched out.

At half time we came in and went over a few things, mostly just reminders on stopping their running game. We were playing pretty well. If Joe hadn't fallen they wouldn't even be on the board. So we didn't have many adjustments to make.

We went back out and I still couldn't get any emotion worked up. That's the first time in my life I've ever been that way in a game of any kind. In the defensive huddle I'd call any defense that popped into my mind and then when the Packers got to the line of scrimmage I'd call an audible. I was acting very blasé about the whole thing. One time I just kept them in the huddle without calling anything and as the Packers were coming up to the line Doug looked at me and said, "What is it? What have you got?"

I looked at him and said as cool as possible, as if I were talking to Nikki and Ricky, "Doug, can't you wait a minute? Wait until they get to the line then I'll see. Don't worry. I'll let you know in plenty of time." He looked at me and shook his head. Very uncharacteristic of me.

For the first time in my life I was treating it like a game. I was just out there to play, I wasn't at war. There were no big emotions, nothing. We were trying to stop Brockington from getting his thousand yards, but hell, he went into the game only needing about thirty.

Then late in the third quarter I got kicked in the head. It was a third-down run, a trap play. The tackle was made and I was on the ground and was kicked in the back of the head. I wasn't completely knocked out, just stunned. I knew where I was, but

I was kind of tipsy. It was fourth down and they were going to punt so I stayed in. I was still trying to recover so I took it easy on the center, Ken Bowman, instead of really hitting him like I usually do.

The idea is that if you give the center a real good belt on the punts, extra points, and field goals, someday you might get him flinching a little and he'll make a bad snap. That's the theory anyway. So I just went through the motions and after the kick walked off the field.

It's a crazy feeling, and I've been through it before. It happened in my first game with the Bears. We were playing an exhibition with the Washington Redskins. It was my first game after the College All-Star game and I was playing alternate quarters with Mike Reilly. He was going the first and third and I'd get my turn in the second and fourth. I was pacing the sidelines, anxious to get my first taste of real professional action.

Finally I got in and on the second or third play I threw a block to cut down a pass receiver at the knees and then everything went black. The next thing I knew I was sitting on the bench going down the line from player to player.

That's Joe. That's Evey. That's Reilly. And calling off their names to myself to make sure I was okay. George Allen was our defensive coach then and he came over and asked me how I was feeling.

"You ready to go again?"

"Yeah, sure," I said as if nothing had happened. "I'm fine."

"What's the score?"

I looked at him kind of funny. "It's nothing to nothing. We're just getting started."

Then he looked at me kind of funny and pointed up at the scoreboard. It took a couple of seconds for it to really sink in, but it was up there in big electric lights. The score was 17–14 and we were in the fourth quarter.

But this time it wasn't that bad. I remember walking off the field and talking to Abe on the sidelines. Then we were back on the field and there was a time-out and I was slowly walking back into our huddle and the Packers were already coming up to the line and Ed was yelling—"What is it? What is it? What's the defense?"

"Hey, go screw yourself. Do anything you want."

And then Doug said, "C'mon Dick, what is it?"

"All right! All right!" And then just as I was starting to call something, POW! the ball was snapped.

Ed and Gary Lyle started hollering over to Abe to get me out. They were down on about our two and everyone was asking me what the defense was so I called, "Sixty-one, Wide, Jill, Lightning." I had invented a new formation.

On the next play, Lyle, the safetyman, lined up a couple of yards deep in the end zone and I went and stood a couple of yards behind him. After the game he told me he was going to say something to me but he figured since I was the defensive captain he'd just let it slide.

Near the end, when I was kind of woozy out there, there was a pileup and they started to fall on my good leg. I felt it cracking. I wasn't that foggy, and I tried to get it out. While I was saving the good leg the other one got caught and it went stiff from then on.

I don't really know how the game ended. I knew we were out on the field. Hell, we're always out on the field. I know I was calling goofy things, defenses, and telling guys "hey, go screw yourself" and acting crazy. I never acted like that before. I never went into a game feeling like I did today.

A few years ago we were playing the Packers in the final game of the season. It was the first year Lombardi stepped down as head coach. We were playing them at home. The Packers were out of it, and if we could beat them we would win the division championship no matter what the Vikings did.

I was so high for that game I could have flown myself to the Coast. It was the first time we had a chance to win something. So the Packers came out and kept completing long bombs on us. Our pass coverage fell completely apart. They way those Packers receivers were so wide open it looked like we were throwing the game.

Some of our guys were laughing about it. That got me so damned mad I wanted to kill a couple of them. Lloyd Phillips was laughing and I almost pushed him off the field.

Boyd Dowler was wide, wide open on one play and Joe Taylor didn't make the tackle until Dowler was inside our ten. We were jogging back and Phillips was laughing and shaking his head and saying, "What the hell's goin' on?"

"What the hell are you laughing about? What's so damn funny?"

"I'm laughing because they're so damn wide open."

"If you were doing your job rushing the passer they wouldn't be so damn wide open."

"Who the hell do you think you are?"

We were arguing right there on the goal line. When we came off the field Joe Fortunato, our defensive coach, asked me what the hell was going on. I told him and then he got mad. I told him if I threw Phillips out of the game he'd know what it was for. He said go ahead and he'd back me all the way.

We ended up losing the damn game 28–27, and I was so goddamn mad I could have bit the goal posts. In the locker room Phillips came over to me and said, "You had a right to do what you did, but I really thought it was funny, their receivers being so wide open all the time."

"Very funny. A big game like this and you're laughing. It's a joke. It's a disgrace and you're part of the disgrace. Laugh that off."

I kept getting madder and madder just listening to the talk around me in the locker room. I heard Phillips and Dick Evey and Larry Rakestraw talking about how they thought they might as well leave for home that night. One guy was driving to Tennessee, another to Georgia, and Phillips to Arkansas.

They must have figured we were going to lose, I thought. Here we are playing for a spot in the playoffs and they must have spent all week packing so they could leave right after the game. That got me so disgusted I could have killed them.

That was a big game. That meant everything. This one meant nothing, just whatever pride we still had that was salvageable. On the defensive team we try to have pride in what we do. We try not to get ourselves disgraced. We want to be able to hold our heads up no matter what happens. But I wonder about some of those guys on the offensive team. On the plane they're the ones who are laughing it up and acting like cutups. If I played that way I'd be too ashamed to show my face anywhere. I'd be too embarrassed to even look at anybody.

31

It's got to the point where I can't even tell anymore if it's the coaches fault or if we're really that bad. When they took Nix out today and put Bobby Douglass in I was beyond caring, way beyond. What the hell, if Dooley wants to cut his own throat that's his business. The only trouble is we get dragged down with him.

When we lost, I used to worry that people would blame us, blame the defense, or blame me. Now it doesn't faze me anymore. It has got to the point where I just don't give a damn what the offense does anymore. They can throw an interception every down, fumble it away every play. I just feel like playing, and if I have to just play for myself that's what I'm going to do.

The game finally came to a close. It was just a case of our offense again not being able to do anything. But we're used to that by now. Usually the guys on the defensive team would be bitching at the offense for not being able to score, but today I guess everyone was just playing for himself. The attitude seemed to be let's do our job and get the game over with. There was no use saying anything to the offense. We're not going to prove anything to anybody so the hell with it. We just slumped into the locker room.

Dooley didn't say anything after the game. I don't think anyone did. I was still a little foggy, a little dizzy, so I took my time shaving and showering. As I was dressing Fuzzy and Paul Hornung came in. We talked about maybe meeting down at the Super Bowl. Fuzzy has also got a place down on Marco Island, Florida, so I told him when I'd be down there and gave him my phone number and told him to give me a call.

Helen was waiting for me and I tried to talk her into going to the party Concannon was having for the team at his joint, the S. O. P., Some Other Place. Jack had lined up prizes for everybody. I don't know where he got them, but there were some really good ones. But Helen said, "No, you go, I'll go home and take the kids off my mother's hands."

At Concannon's the bitching that didn't get finished in the locker room started up all over again. Most of the defensive players sat together; Doug and George Seals and Lyle and O'Bradovich. O'B could barely make it. His knee was screwed up. His ribs were banged up and he got his neck twisted. He looked like the Hunchback of Notre Dame.

Doug said he was going to leave for sure. He and Seals and Concannon and Gordon and a couple more guys had all played out their options. But the way Pete Rozelle handles these things no team hardly wants to touch a guy, he makes them give up so much in exchange.

Shinnick was talking about looking for a job somewhere else. So just to get into things with the rest of the guys I said I thought I'd try to get the Old Man to trade me. I said maybe I'd go to the Super Bowl and talk to some coaches or an owner or general manager. It'd have to be someone with a little guts, someone like Joe Robbie at Miami or Al Davis at Oakland or Lou Saban, or a maverick like Mecom of the Saints.

We sat around having a few drinks and telling each other how we were going to miss the other guys when we were playing the Super Bowl next year. And someone, I think it was Lyle, said, "Hell, you have a Super Bowl fourteen times a year—every payday." Old Gary really cut loose on his hero then, telling everyone that I paid more in taxes than he made in salary.

Then he started telling everybody about the things I was saying in the huddle and how I was acting on the field. They were all laughing like hell. It was either the way Lyle was telling it or maybe they didn't expect me to act that way on the field. For me it was really stepping out of character. I'm always supposed to be so serious. Maybe it was a combination of both Lyle's storytelling and my usual image.

He was making with the imitations—"Relax Doug, relax. When I think it's time for you to know I'll tell you."

Then he started with all the wild calls, like Sixty-one, Wide, Jill, Lightning, and how I lined up behind him on the goal line. Everyone thought that was funny as hell, and I had to laugh at myself.

"You haven't seen it all yet," Doug told Bru and Moore and a couple of the other younger guys. "Wait till he starts calling some of those wonderful time-outs of his."

"Well if you guys would get in shape I wouldn't have to call so many time-outs. Looking out for you guys is another one of my responsibilities, you know."

33

"Yeah, like with about twenty seconds to go."

Then Doug started telling the story of the game I called a time-out with hardly any time on the clock. We were playing Detroit. They were beating us. They had the ball on about our twenty-five or so. We had no chance. They just ran a play and were standing in the huddle to let the clock run out.

I walked up to the referee and asked, "How many time-outs do we have left?" He looked at me kind of funny and then said, "Two."

"Okay, I want one," I told him.

"You don't want any time-out," he said shaking his head.

"Look, I have them coming and I want one. I need one. I'm calling time-out."

"All right," he said, and blew his little whistle. "You got a time-out."

During this little argument the guys in our huddle are bitching—"C'mon let's get the hell out of here. What the hell do we want to stand out here for"—and the guys in Detroit huddle, they were really bitching. They thought I was going nuts. "Hey what the hell's the matter with you. Let's get the hell out of here."

"Listen, I got my reasons. I needed that time-out," I told our guys. So we all lined up again and the Lions ran another play. Munson fell on the ball, or something like that, and we all ran off the field.

Everybody forgot about it for a while, but just before we were going to leave the locker room Doug asked, "Say, why the hell did you call that time-out?"

"To get one more shot at Flanagan," I told him. He burst out laughing. So did everyone at the table.

It was a good party. At least it helped us to forget what a sorry spectacle we were out there today. They had dance contests and Bill Tucker and Nancy Staley and Nancy O'Bradovich and Ernie Polus, a friend of Ed's, were in the finals. The team of Tucker and Staley won $100. Jim Grabowski and his wife, Suzy, won $100 in the Charleston contest. I was sort of glad Jim won something. He's been in Dooley's doghouse lately and he hasn't been playing at all after he started the season doing a helluva job. The Packers cut him during summer camp and he really wanted to get a shot at them.

After the food and dancing they had the drawings for the door prizes. First they'd announce the prize and then Joy Piccolo pulled out the winning names. They had some big cash prizes. Bobby Douglass won $250. Fig Newton won $200. Lyle won $150. Willie Holman won the grand prize, a five-day trip to Las Vegas.

Doug and I were trying to guess who the winners were going to be before Joy pulled the name out. We were each right about once in forty tries. They got down near the end and one of the last prizes was a television set. "I got a feeling one of us is going to win it," Doug said.

"All right," I said, "let's start walking up to get it." They called Doug's name. I won a damn hot comb.

The party lasted well into the early hours and I was one of the last to leave. I told Helen I'd be home early. I should have said what day. At about three o'clock I went out into the morning carrying my hot comb and a little kiddie football outfit I was awarded as a bonus.

3

Monday, December 13

It was after nine when I got up, and then I gave Helen her assignments for the day—go to the bank, take her mother home, and an assortment of other errands. I have to clean the furnace filter, fix the hot water heater, and check out the freezer so that everything will be in perfect shape for us to leave next week. And watch Big Matt. Helen put him to sleep before she left.

How the hell could we have played that bad?

Had to sit around and wait for that guy to call me about my camper. I took it out to a Chevy dealer in Highland, Indiana, Friday to have him put bigger tires on it and the guy was supposed to call me today. I wanted to get it back home so I could start packing.

It's as if nobody was even trying. It's as if nobody cared. Getting beat like that. By a team like that.

What's more frustrating than waiting for some guy to call? A watched phone never rings. To kill some time I called Jay McGreevy and jagged him about staying here in the cold. Jay is president of Remco, distributors of kitchen appliances. He uses a lot of guys on the team as well as Stan Mikita and Bobby Hull and other Black Hawks for advertising and promotion.

It's humiliating. I don't even want to show my face. People see you and give you that "it's not your fault crap." Glad I don't have to go anywhere today.

Actually I was hoping he wouldn't be there. I forgot his home address and I just wanted to get it from his secretary so I could send him a thank-you note for the surprise birthday party he had for me last Thursday. Just some friends and a lavish dinner. Old Jay really knows how to lay it on. I got some nice gifts and they had a papier-mâché helmet made for me the size of a small swimming pool. "Hope we didn't get too small a size" the tag said. Everybody had a good time.

Jay was trying to tell me I shouldn't go to Florida. "It won't be a white Christmas," he said. "The hell it won't," I told him. "We've got miles of the most beautiful white sand beach you've ever seen."

He said he had some more of my pictures and instructional football books he wanted me to sign for his customers. I told him I'd probably see him Friday. I had to go down that way anyway to get some of my records from Fox. I like Fox, but I think I could go an awfully long time without seeing him and never miss him.

I could feel my knee. I could feel the cast around it. I could feel it throbbing.

I'll never forget the day, January 29, 1971. Fox (Dr. Theodore Fox, Bears team doctor) said I'd only be on the table for about an hour. They wheeled me in about eight and it was close to noon when they brought me out. The cartilage was loose and all the ligaments were torn. Some fragments had worked their way in between the knee joints. I used to give the boys a kick by lifting the top of my leg right off the knee.

I talked to everyone I knew who had a knee problem. I asked them every question I could think of and listened to everything they told me. Nothing prepared me for what I went through.

A couple of days after the operation I started getting pains. They were sharp and constant right through the entire leg, from hip to foot. I'd call Fox and tell him and he'd give me a prescription for more painkillers and sleeping pills. A week later I went in for my first cast change and to have some of the stitches removed. They had the leg in hyperextension. It was too straight. It's as if you were sitting down and put your heel on another chair and then put a heavy weight on the knee.

They thought maybe that was one reason for the pain. Everything looked fine when they took the stitches out. I told them about the pain, but they couldn't account for it any other way. There was a streaky red mark on the outside of my knee. They thought maybe the cast was too tight. It was numb there. So they put on a new cast and let me bend the knee just a hair. I went back home, but the pain came back with me.

Nothing helped. I couldn't sleep, I couldn't read, I couldn't get my mind off it. The bed was too soft so I moved to the couch. Then one night it started to throb. It felt like it was going to explode right through the cast.

I called Fox. It was about ten thirty and he told me to meet him at the hospital. Somehow I staggered to the car and my brother-in-law Glenn drove me those fifty miles to the Illinois Masonic Hospital. They wheeled me in and cut away the top half of the cast. Then they shot me with double and triple doses of painkillers and tranquilizers.

The next morning when the nurse was removing the tape strips that anchor the plaster the scar was all scabby and something was trying to burst through the incision. They called Fox and ran some culture tests. They found I was allergic to the gut they used. Some of it was finally starting to dissolve and the pus was running out.

The poison had traveled all the way from my foot to the lymph nodes in the groin. There was pain, the same sharp, hot pain like getting stung by a Portuguese man-of-war, streaking from my toes to my hip. There was a small hole in the incision and Fox tried to open it a little more and work some of the stuff out. Then they put me in another cast and sent me home.

Every six days I'd return to the hospital for a cast change and the stuff would be all inside the cast and down my leg. The stink was horrible. I thought my leg was dead. They told me it was good that it was coming out, but I developed a rash down my leg, and I wanted to go through the ceiling every time Fox stuck his cotton swap under the skin. Finally they removed the cast for good and I started soaking the knee in the whirlpool to loosen the adhesions.

After about a week I got a certain amount of bend in the knee and then it stiffened up completely. I went back to Fox. He drained it with a giant needle and then shot something into it. A few hours after I got home there was another attack. It started throbbing. Hot pains were flashing through my entire leg. I went back to popping painkillers and sleeping pills, but it was midnight before I dozed off.

In the morning the scab was real loose. I kept pressing it and then a piece of suture over an inch long, just like a fish line, came wiggling out. But I couldn't stop. I kept pressing it and sweating ice water.

I called Fox and told him, and when I went to see him again we thought we had it all out. But we'd go a little while and it'd all come back. I couldn't get my leg bent because of the internal swelling, so they decided to reopen it and clean it out for good. He reoperated March 29. I spent four more weeks in a cast.

I can still feel that hot sun. The first of July already and I was just starting to run, just starting to jog. Camp only a couple of weeks off. Had to exercise it for weeks first, hours every day. The whirlpool, the weight boot. Extend. Extend. Extend. Little by little it bent, it extended. The knee became a separate entity. A life and will of its own. C'mon knee. Let's go. Straighten out. Straighten out. Scream at it. Sweat, as much from the fear of reinjury as from effort. You get to know your body when you work with it every day. And your mind. How they work together, conspire, lie to you, try to get you to take it easy, to quit, to plant the suggestion and fear of reinjury.

My body's my trade. It's my only asset. My only tool. I've gotten to know it. I know how much it can take and how much further I can push it when it wants me to quit. So I fool it. When I'm running and my knee starts to tell me to take it easy I play a little game to distract my mind. I imagine I have the ball and I'm running for the winning touchdown. Or I imagine I'm chasing

39

the runner and if I don't catch him and tackle him we'll lose. Or I imagine I'm the field announcer and I introduce the starting lineup.

At left end . . . from South Carolina State . . . Six-four, Two hundred and fifty pounds . . . Number eighty-five, Willie Holman. Raaaaaaaaaa. Under the goal posts and up the field.
At left tackle . . . from the University of Missouri . . . Six-three, two hundred and sixty pounds . . . Number sixty-seven, George Seals. Raaaaaaaaaa. Seals rumbles upfield. He and Willie give each other welcoming thumps.
When I come to my own name I hear a tremendous roar— Rrrrr aaaaaaaaaaaaaaaaaaaaaa—that drowns out the introduction. Try and act unaffected. The chalk marks sail by.

I go through the entire team. Sometimes I do the offense too, and sometimes even the opposition. Sometimes I imagine we're playing away from home. The cheers turn into boos and name calling and a shower of verbal, liquid, and cardboard abuse.

Baltimore is one of my favorite towns. The fans wait for us at the players' entrance and as soon as we start getting off the bus they let us have it. One time a priest rode to the park with us and when they saw him getting off they let him have it too.

"Hey, they brought their own priest. They'll need a priest. Hey father, gonna give 'em the last rites? God ain't gonna do you guys any good today." That's just the mild stuff.

That priest might have heard that kind of language before, but I doubt if he ever had such a concentrated barrage directed at him before. At that time it was still quite an experience for me. Now, hell, if I went somewhere and didn't get it I'd be disappointed.

We beat them that day. We shut them out. As I was coming off the field with the game ball in my hands they were screaming down at us. I threw the ball up to one of them, but I made sure I didn't throw it high enough for him to catch it. I was hoping he'd fall out of the stands trying to reach it. I laughed at him and kept going right into the locker room.

The milkman jogged me back to real life when he dropped off

the usual two gallons. He asked for Ricky because he usually gives him a couple of cartons of chocolate milk.

I'm glad he stopped by. He was somebody to talk to, somebody to help me take my mind off myself.

This has to be my toughest, most frustrating year in football. When I got to camp I still couldn't run and every day I got up early and went down to the basement and lifted my leg on the weight machine. After breakfast I'd go out to practice and then lift again before lunch. Take a little nap, then back to the weight machine, and then out to practice again. Practice was the toughest thing. Not the work, the not being able to work.

Everyone else was out there working and there was nothing I could do but stand around and watch. I couldn't make any kind of cut at all. All I could do was jog in a straight line. I started pushing the dummy and the two-man sled. Just pushing it slowly, pushing off with each leg, trying to get the strength back gradually.

Howard Mudd and I were sort of rooming together. Sort of, I say, because he had a knee problem too, but it wasn't coming around, and they wouldn't let him move in exactly because they were pretty sure he wouldn't be able to come back. Howard and I hit it off real well since he came here a couple of years ago from the 49ers in a trade for Rosey Taylor. That's saying a lot for Howard.

He helped me a lot. He showed me different things about lifting weights and how to improve the knee. This was his third knee operation and he knew most of the tricks. Lifting can become a terrible bore. It's a real grind when you have to do it on your own, and Howard was my sole companion in misery.

We were always on the sidelines. We were never part of anything. You feel like you have some unspeakable disease. No one talks to you and you feel you have nothing to talk to them about. I got the feeling I was cheating on the rest of the team. All the guys were hitting the sleds, running the sprints, scrimmaging, gasping and dying in the heat and humidity and there I was standing, watching on the sidelines. I wanted to beg Abe to give me something to do, anything. Let me hold the dummies.

Howard was good for me. We both had our knee problems

and we were both working together. We could cheer each other on. The thing that kept my spirits up was that little by little, day by day, I could feel myself improving.

But Howard wasn't. Finally they sent him back to Fox for still another operation and gave him his release. He was at the party at Jay's the other night. He's going to law school and is an assistant coach at the University of California now and he's melted himself down to about two hundred pounds. A little light for a guard.

The exhibition season was just about over before I finally got in a game. I went the first half against the Oilers in the Astrodome in Houston. I had the knee taped up real good.

I started taping both knees after I got my right one banged up in our first league game the year before against the New York Giants. I had already pulled the hamstring in that leg in an exhibition game with Denver and really got the knee banged up against the Giants.

After that Shinnick told me I better start taping the left one too. He said there is a natural tendency to put more pressure on the good knee.

Thinking back I know it was just a matter of time, the years of getting hit from the side and clipped were catching up to me. That first game, the Giants game, I got hit from the side again and that put the finish to the knee. I think it was their tight end on a screen pass.

I was trying to fight off the Giants' center, Greg Larson, when someone came across and threw a cross-body block.

The first thing that hit my mind was—it's all over. After all these years the knee was already loose and it was simply a matter of time until it was going to get completely knocked out. As I was getting up I was waiting for it to buckle the way Gale Sayers' had, but it didn't. It kept getting weaker and weaker and it was really hurting me so they taped it at half time and I made it through the end of the game. After that it was just a week-by-week deal.

Fox said we'd just wait until it got knocked out completely. What the hell, we only had thirteen games left. But I always knew it would happen someday. I started having trouble with it in high school. I'd even have to be careful going down stairs.

When they opened the leg after the 1970 season they found they could swing it sideways about four centimeters. A good one will only go about a half, or at the most one centimeter. Mine was kind of like a gate. That's the field test, to try to swing the leg sideways. When a man is down the doctor will try it on him. If it moves a little and then grabs they know it's a partial tear. Mine was going all the way. It seemed like ninety degrees, as if only the skin was keeping it on.

The first time I was on the field for 1971 was against the Oilers and wouldn't you know it, the very first play they came right at me and I had to make a tackle. I felt all right. That was a relief, but I didn't have any flex in the knee. When the ball was snapped and play was in progress I managed to get my mind off the damn knee and concentrate on the ball.

But as the half wore on it gradually tired. That was natural from the little bit of practice I was able to get in, and I still hadn't run full speed. So I sat out the second half and then we came back to Chicago to play Denver in our final exhibition.

I thought that would be a good test because with Floyd Little and Bob Anderson they have a good running game. It still felt strong going into the third quarter and I was tempted to push it a little and play the fourth quarter. But I told myself I better not because we opened the regular season with the Pittsburgh Steelers the following week.

During the week I tried to do everything I possibly could to get in shape to go the whole game. I was lifting weights every day and running up and down the stadium steps. I was anxious and impatient to get it in shape, but I didn't think that sometimes it needed rest as much as it needed work.

Thursday night of that week I put some weight on my right leg as I was going down the stairs and a hot pain shot through it. That scared me. It hurt every time I took a step. I called Fox. He said it was nothing, but I better stop by at his office Friday before going to practice. The ligament was being irritated. The best thing, and the only thing for it, he said, was rest. Just lay off it for a while.

I went to practice and tried to run, but I couldn't even jog.

43

I couldn't even walk fast. So there I was, just leaning against the goal post watching the other guys practice and here it was only two days before the game.

I just wanted to go away and hide and cry. I felt everything was washing away, that I'd never be ready, that I might not play at all this season. I felt a bone-deep powerlessness.

Saturday I was just able to jog a little bit. No kind of speed. I told Fox and he told me to stay off it. All that night I just dozed and kept waking up. I lay there, flat on my back, afraid to get up, afraid to put any kind of weight on my leg.

You play this game and you're in shape and young and you can feel your strength. You think you're indestructible, immortal almost, and then something like this happens and you learn about pain and fear and frailty. It scares you almost out of your mind.

Game day came and it felt a little better. I asked Fox if he was going to put anything in there. He said he'd rather wait until after the pre-game warm-up. So I went out there thinking, if it works, fine. If it doesn't, well, I'll just have to sit one out. That's what I was telling myself, but inside I was nervous and worried and I was so sensitive in that direction that I thought every nerve was running right down to my knee.

The weather at least was on my side. It was a rainy day, a misty day. I was glad of that because it made the Astroturf a little slipperier. To me that was very important. That Astroturf is miserable stuff.

It's great for the fans who sit up there and see this neat, almost immaculate field. But next time you're up there just remember that under that thin green rug is a skinny sheet of sponge rubber and then rock-hard asphalt. Worst of all, there's no give. Plant your foot to make a cut or make a block or a tackle and your foot stops immediately. There's no skid.

It sends a shock right up your knee, your weakest piece of bodily equipment. But with the mist and dampness on the field we could get a little slide, instead of knee-shuddering jarring stops.

The early birds went out there, Buffone, Brupbacher, myself, Mac, and Bobby Joe Green practicing his punts. We were throwing the ball and shagging the kicks and fooling around. I ran backward a little and it felt pretty good. When I jogged forward a little the pain was hardly there. My knee was feeling better.

I went back into the locker room before anyone else and Fox asked me how it felt. I told him it felt fairly strong and that the pain seemed to leave it as it got loosened up. We decided it wasn't necessary to shoot it. We just taped it up. So with five quarters of exhibition play under my belt I went out to play the Pittsburgh Steelers.

It was the first game and we both wanted it real bad. Everybody wants to get that first game. It sets you up in a positive mental attitude right away and gets you looking forward to the next game instead of looking backward and asking yourself, why?, and what you should have done differently. You worked hard to get this far, and if you blow it you feel like all that work was wasted and you have to start over again.

Our defense was really up. I don't see how we could have played much better. We made a few mistakes, but nothing really major. And, most important, we were getting the turnovers, taking the ball away from the Steelers and giving it to our offense in great field position.

I intercepted one pass on a screen play Terry Bradshaw called, but it was nullified because we were offside. On the very next play Bradshaw threw one over the middle and I guess he wasn't reading our defense right because I grabbed that one too. I got another one later and just missed a fourth when I slipped going for the ball.

We had Bradshaw confused all day. We kept showing him different formations, and every series we'd switch from full zone to man-to-man to blitz. We didn't give him a chance to pick up any tendencies.

Going into the fourth quarter we were still behind 14–3. The offense just couldn't get anything going. Pittsburgh had the ball and were running an end sweep with John Fuqua. O'Bradovich hit him high and hard and knocked the ball loose. Bru scooped it up and ran about thirty yards for the touchdown.

That really set the defense on fire, but there were just about two minutes left. As we were standing along the sidelines for the kickoff Abe told me that they'd probably try to kill the clock with some traps. He told me if I could see it coming to go ahead and blitz, we might force another fumble.

They were inside their own thirty and I knew Bradshaw wasn't going to throw the ball if he could help it. I had one of those intuitive visions. While they were still in the huddle I could see the play.

They tried to run a trap. Their center, Ray Mansfield, moved to his left to block Bill Staley and I shot right up the hole. For a split second I thought I could get the hand-off. I hit Warren Bankston just as hard as I could the instant he touched the ball. It popped loose and we got it. Kent Nix came in off the bench and threw it in for the winning touchdown.

That was so satisfying I can't begin to express it. Two days before the game I couldn't walk, and then to have it come out like that. The perfect play for me is to hit the ball-carrier and have him fumble and then recover the fumble myself.

That's perfection. Just making a good, solid tackle is hard enough. You've always got guys blocking you and grabbing you and holding. If they ever started calling all the holding that goes on they'd just keep walking right out of the stadium. And most backs are too smart to give you that good, solid shot. They know how to twist and feint and how to avoid direct contact as much as possible.

I know that guy in *Playboy* magazine wrote a story about a year ago in which I was supposed to have said that the perfect tackle I see in my dreams is to hit a guy so hard his head flies off and rolls back toward his own goal line. That's a lot of crap. I never dream about knocking anyone's head off.

When I was a kid I used to fantasize about great plays on the field; running for touchdowns, throwing passes, winning games on long field goals. But it's a funny thing, I never dreamt about being a Bear or a Colt or a Ram and performing these great deeds in Yankee Stadium or the Coliseum or Wrigley Field. All my fantasies involved me at my own level of play. I never projected myself into a different time or a different situation.

It was always about me where I was then, at that moment. Then at Illinois, when I began to play mostly defense, my daydreams all centered around some extraordinary defensive play.

I tackle the guy. He fumbles. I pick up the ball and run it in for a touchdown. It can happen.

In the Pittsburgh game someone else recovered the ball. But in the Green Bay game, the first Green Bay game, with us trailing in the last couple of minutes, I shot the gap and hit Dave Hampton. He fumbled and I recovered. We went in for the tying touchdown. Now that gave me a helluva lot of satisfaction. So did catching the game-winning extra point against Washington.

We had just scored very late in the game to tie the Redskins and I went in to block for the extra point that would put us in front. Now these things are pretty routine. An extra point is hardly ever missed.

Douglass was holding for Percival and I was blocking on the left wing. There was a bad snap and Douglass picked up the ball and starting running backward. Most of the Redskins were chasing him and he was circling and dodging and giving ground all the time.

I figured, hell, there's no use trying to block because I'd never get there in time to do him any good. So I just thought of getting open. I was an eligible receiver because I lined up in the backfield.

I drifted toward the goal post and then cut and started running for the deep left corner of the end zone. By this time Douglass was back to the thirty or thirty-five and just as he was about to be swarmed under he let it fly.

He saw me just in time. I went up and caught the ball and we had a win. There was no way I could fantasize that one— not a forty-yard extra point catch.

The guys gave me the game ball after the Steeler game and I took two balls and gave one to Fox and one to Dr. Jerry Kolb, his associate. A lot of the guys kid Fox and Kolb about how they can't wait to get everybody on the table, and how they want to use any excuse to start cutting, and about guys who never make it back or who have problems, but I felt I owed them a lot. I don't think that mine was an ordinary operation. The knee was pretty well screwed up before I went in there, and football is my life.

Everything depended on my knee and the doctors getting it fixed. In a lot of ways it's a wonder I did get to play. I just had to play. Although I'm frustrated after this lousy season I still have to be satisfied. I have to think I can look forward to next year.

Then Matt woke up and I had to change his pants and it's a real struggle because he doesn't like anybody messing with him. I made him some Jello water and I was still sitting around waiting for that call from that Chevy guy. Finally I just got tired of waiting so I said, the hell with it, dressed Matt, and took him for a walk to my mother's.

She lives just two houses away, so I can walk across our lawn, our neighbors' lawn, and be there. I let Matt walk around outside for a while. It was a nice day. He's really a great kid. He's about ten months now and has been walking about a month already. He walks around with both hands up over his head, just like someone told him to stick 'em up. He waddled around after some birds and inspected some trees and then we went in.

My mother started telling me that she heard Mike Pyle say that O'B was going to get a Cadillac for his day. Pyle played center for us for years and now he does a post-game radio show where listeners call up and ask him questions and criticize the way the game was played and the strategy we used. They still don't know our strategy is to run three plays and punt. That way we can wear down the other team's offense while ours will still be fresh.

For some reason or other that irritated me, I kind of snapped at her and told her that was a lot of crap, that she shouldn't believe everything she reads or hears. I told her they were just going to have a Cadillac outside the stadium to advertise Ed's day.

Then she said that some caller told Pyle they ought to trade me and get some running backs and offensive linemen. And Pyle said no, they couldn't do that, and started to give a lot of reasons why. If he only knew.

4

Tuesday, December 14

Talked to the kids about Florida again on the way to school. That's all I seem to be able to think of. It was a damp, misty, chilly, windy day and I was telling them, just think, in just seven more days we'll be in the sun again and in the ocean every day.

Both Nikki and Ricky have been swimming for over a year now. They took lessons at a pool around here and when we're down in Florida they can't get enough of the water. They love it, the swimming and diving and jumping off the board. I can't wait to see how Big Matt takes to the water.

When I got home Vern Buhl called. We talked for a while about the Rams-Redskins game the night before, and about George Allen.

Vern was my baby-sitter when I was drafted by the Bears in 1964. Each team put someone they could trust to watch over their draft choices so the other league wouldn't steal them. Vern was mine, or to put it more accurately, I was his responsibility.

Actually the Bears were the last team I thought would draft me. They hadn't contacted me at all. Denver had talked to me prior to the draft. So I was really surprised when I heard the Bears were planning on taking me, especially after the telegram they sent my line coach, Burt Ingwersen.

Burt called me into the coach's office a couple of days before I went to Chicago for a meeting with the Bears. He said he got a telegram from George Allen saying I slowed down since my junior year and couldn't get back on pass coverage. That's a bad rap I've had to live with since.

Burt was very upset. He had played with Halas as one of the original Decatur Staleys and as an original Chicago Bear. He said he couldn't believe they would send a telegram like that. He was so mad he tore it up and threw it away, but he just wanted me to know about it and what they said about me before I went to talk contract with them.

Denver had some people at my last college game against Michigan State. Neither of us had much to play for as teams, but Dick Gordon and Grabowski went into the game just a couple of yards apart for the Big Ten rushing title. Grabowski had a big day, over two hundred yards I think, and we pretty much stopped Gordon.

Late in the fourth quarter they drove downfield and made a first down on our one. We had them shut out and I was determined nobody was going to score on me my last game. Three straight plays I made the tackle and on fourth down I threw the runner for a loss, and made him fumble. Burt always said I ought to get the tape of that game, that it was the greatest goal line sequence he'd ever seen. But I never did, just one more thing I'll probably regret about twenty years from now.

After the game the Denver people took me to their hotel suite where I talked to the owner, Gerald H. Phipps, on the telephone. Phipps told me they wanted me very much. He didn't make any offers over the phone, but he said he'd see me later in the week. He had an appointment with my attorney Arthur Morse.

Morse, a Chicago lawyer and sports promoter who had helped other athletes negotiate pro contracts, was recommended by my head coach, Pete Elliott, and our athletic director, Doug Mills.

I finally heard from the Bears the Thursday after the Michigan State game, and went to Chicago on Friday. We had meetings scheduled with the Bears and Phipps for the same day.

We met with Phipps first in Morse's office. He had an offer all written out and broken down; I'd save this much, they'd invest so much, and I'd have so much for living expenses. Morse stopped him in the middle of his presentation.

"Look," he said, "we certainly appreciate your idea of being concerned about Dick's future Mr. Phipps, but we'd like to have some say in how his affairs are handled. It's really not necessary for you to plan all these programs for him. We have a few ideas of our own on how we should set up an investment program for him."

That set Phipps back a bit. He said something else and then named a figure. As I recall it was less than $100,000. They wanted a three-year contract, and he stuck out his hand and said, "Is it a deal?"

Morse said, "Well, we can't shake on it because we haven't heard from the Bears yet. It wouldn't be fair to Dick if we didn't at least give them the courtesy of listening to what they had to say."

We really had no intention of signing with Denver. Morse wanted a big city, but what most concerned us at that time was whether or not the American Football League was going to be in business in a few years. It sounds funny now to even say that. But that's also the reason he didn't want Grabowski, who he negotiated for the following year, going to Miami, although they offered Jim a helluva deal. It turns out that Morse was a helluva negotiator but not too much of a prophet.

The only AFL city that looked right to Morse and to me was New York. Morse knew Sonny Werblin, a real shrewd dealer who owned the Jets. He was trying to get Werblin to trade Denver for my draft rights. He figured that if Denver knew I wasn't going to go for them under any circumstances they'd be inclined to deal with Werblin.

We said good-bye to Phipps and went over to the Bears' office. That's the first time I met the Old Man, George Halas, Sr., a man I'd heard about and read about all my life.

I didn't form any real impressions of the Old Man at that first meeting. I just knew I was in the presence of THE MAN. To me Halas was the man who represented the power and the prestige of the National Football League.

His son, Muggs, the president of the club, and Allen, who was then defensive coach and director of player personnel, were also there. The five of us were sitting in the office making small talk until finally Allen tried to get things rolling.

"Well Dick, we think you're a great player with a great future and we'd love to have you in our organization."

"If that's what you think why did you send that telegram to Burt Ingwersen?"

Tact wasn't always my strong point, but I wasn't being smart about it either. I was still young and didn't know how to broach these things diplomatically. I still don't. But I wanted to know for sure where I stood with them and what they really thought of me.

"Well, in this telegram you said I'm not very good on pass coverage, and now you're telling me how great I am."

The Old Man looked at Allen and asked, "What is this, George?"

Allen said it was probably just the regular telegram they send to players they're interested in drafting. Then he kind of mumbled something and said he had them all on file.

Morse got into it—"If you have it on record why not get a copy then we can all take a look at it so we can clear this up right now."

Halas must not have known anything about it because he said, "Yeah, George, go get it."

Allen left and Halas was saying how this must all be some sort of mistake, a misunderstanding. He said they thought highly enough of me to make me their number one draft pick. He repeated what Allen said about sending telegrams to all the players they're interested in drafting.

Allen came back a couple of minutes later without the telegram. He looked a little sheepish and blamed the secretary. He said she either misplaced it or threw it away by mistake.

Morse looked from face to face and then said, "All right, this is what we want." He gave them a figure well over a couple of hundred thousand. I just hoped that no one heard me gulp.

The Old Man kind of smacked his lips and said they'd have to talk about it. As they were going out of the room for a conference Morse said, "Can you make it quick? Dick has to go to New York for a TV program." Morse's cheek always amazed me, but I was supposed to go to New York to tape the Johnny Carson show as a member of the Kodak All-American team.

Halas came back in a few minutes and said they'd need more time to work something out. We said that was fine. When we got downstairs Morse told me not to discuss what had gone on with the Bears and Denver with anyone not even Bill Taylor who was going with me. When I got to New York Vern Buhl introduced himself and told me it was his job to stay with me. He said if I wanted anything I should just let him know. I said okay. If they wanted to throw their money around like that it was all right with me.

Snow held up the plane and we got in too late for the taping session anyway. We checked in at the Waldorf. Just about all the players were there with their baby-sitters.

Everybody went out on the town that night. A mob of us piled into Basin Street East and just about took over the joint. Craig Morton was going from joint to joint with about five other guys. He kept grabbing everybody's tab and signing the Dallas Cowboys. His sitter didn't care. Hell, if Craig would have bought the saloon that night that probably would have been all right too.

We had a good time, at least from what I can remember of it it was a good time. But it wasn't as wild as the stories that were being written in those days about guys being plied with broads and booze to get them to sign, or owners running up with handfuls of money, and no one that I heard of was kidnapped and kept locked in a hotel room. We just cut loose among ourselves. For the first time in our lives we felt a definite change. I suppose it's the way you're supposed to feel when you graduate from one level of life to another. Maybe we even got a little rowdy.

When I got back to the hotel there was a message from Morse who said that Halas had called and wanted to talk some more. He told me he'd keep me informed.

Saturday was the draft, and I didn't feel like sitting around the hotel all day, and I didn't want my chaperon with me either, even though Vern was not supposed to let me out of his sight. So I pulled a little fast one on him.

I called Mike Taliaferro and told him to come right over and pick me up. Mike was our quarterback at Illinois when we went to the Rose Bowl. He graduated the year before and was now playing for the Jets. He told me I'd really like it there.

He drove me to Shea Stadium and showed me around. Then I had a meeting with Werblin and the coach, Weeb Ewbank. We didn't talk money. They just said they'd love to have me.

By the time I got back the draft was over. When I walked in

Buhl looked relieved to see me. He said the Bears had picked me and that Halas had been calling all afternoon. The Old Man would ask where I was and Vern kept telling him I was there, but unfortunately I couldn't come to the phone just then. He blamed it on some bad food the night before and a change in water.

We were just making small talk waiting for the Old Man or Morse to call when Vern made a little confession. He said he was responsible for the scouting report that led to the telegram to Ingwersen.

"What the hell did you do that for?"

"Well, it was after the Northwestern game and you didn't have a very good first half."

"But I had a helluva second half."

"Yeah, I know," he said, and shrugged and smiled.

"You sure started a lot of trouble. I was blaming Allen."

Morse called a few minutes later and said the Bears had agreed to everything. "All right," I told him, "tell them it's a deal."

That night the Jets came around to do some more talking, but I said sorry. Later I found out that Werblin was playing a waiting game. He was trying to get the biggest name he could to commit to the Jets. Everyone knew that a strong New York franchise would make the league that much stronger. It paid off for him. He got Denver to give him their number one pick and he took Joe Namath. He knew what he was doing, and so did Namath.

A funny thing happened then. At least it seemed funny to me. Lamar Hunt had just come in from Kansas City. He got hold of me and for some reason or other he wanted me to talk to Gale Sayers to get him to sign with the Chiefs.

Hunt must have thought that New York had closed a deal with me and that I was sewed up for the AFL. I found out later that's what the deal was supposed to be. The league was fighting for prestige. They hadn't done too well in signing name players in the past, so this year they were supposed to sign a player for any team he wanted and straighten things out later.

Anyway I didn't know Sayers. I only met him once or twice, and only casually at that. I didn't know what I could say to him or anyone else about signing with one team or another. I figured

54

that was something for everyone to decide for himself. I told Hunt I didn't see how I could possibly do what he asked, and besides I had agreed to sign with the Bears.

Down in the hospitality suite I saw Sayers and he was all smiles. "I've signed," he said. "I'm going with the Bears."

"That's good," I told him. "I'm signing with the Bears myself."

Tom Nowatzke was one of the first guys to actually sign his contract. Detroit grabbed him. Now he was kind of nervous about it. He thought maybe he signed too quickly. Maybe he could have gotten more if he waited a little while. He was asking everyone what kind of offers they were getting so he could compare.

Maybe I signed too quickly too. Maybe I could have got more. But hell, I was so anxious to play pro ball I would have accepted almost anything. It's a good thing the Bears didn't know that. It seemed like a good deal to me. I wanted the NFL and the Bears had won the championship in 1963. I was with a winner.

At that time I thought, and it was the accepted thinking, that the American League was the inferior league. Whether it was or not was immaterial. That's how the majority of the public thought of it too. I wanted to prove myself in the toughest possible competition. If I had gone to the AFL and become a star some people would say "so what?" I wouldn't have proved anything, or so I thought then.

It was a good deal. It was probably the best contract a lineman ever got and maybe the best of the year. Namath would have had to get that $400,000 to beat it. and I understand his contained a lot of "If's."

Anyway, I made a few friends, and that's something money can't buy, not real ones anyway, like Vern Buhl. I still kid him about the hard time I gave him when he was my baby-sitter, and I tease him about how cheap he was.

He was Grabowski's baby-sitter the following year and the Packers put a Lear jet at their disposal. They traveled to New York and Florida on it. So I still tell him, "Sure, you took Grabo to all those New York shows and on a nice Florida vacation. All I ever got out of you was a lousy dollar cigar."

We visit back and forth and go out to dinner now and then. Vern's still a big Bears supporter. He still does a little scouting.

He's someone I can lean on a little, do some bitching to, and know that whatever I say is not going to go any further.

When I was watching the Rams-Redskins game last night and looking at Allen and what he's done with that team in one year, how well drilled and well disciplined they are, it crossed my mind that I remembered Dooley or one of the other coaches saying how they ran Allen out of Chicago a few years ago.

I was thinking, boy, they really showed him. They sure ran him out. He became a successful coach at Los Angeles. Although he didn't win the big games he still had a helluva won-lost record. He built up the crowds out there and had a tremendous personal salary.

Then he went to Washington and got a piece of the action, a free hand in running the team, and he's built them into an instant contender. Now they're in the playoffs. And I was thinking, yeah, that Dooley really showed Allen. He really ran him out of town. Allen must still be thanking him. I'd like to find some enemies like that.

For some reason the park district picked today to fix the wiring and heating in the locker rooms. They couldn't wait until after practice. We had to dress in the dark and it was cold in there.

It reminded me of what happened in the Wrigley Field locker room toward the end of last season. It started with a smell that kept getting stronger. It was right in our locker area. I thought it was Doug, and he probably thought it was me. If it wasn't Doug I thought it could be Bob Hyland.

Finally one day I told Doug, "You're wearing those goddamn gym shoes with no socks and your feet stink. Look how dirty those shoes are."

He said his wife told him he ought to wash them, and the next day I noticed they were clean. But the smell was still there, even stronger. I thought maybe it was me after all. I caught Hyland sniffing around in his locker. Everybody around there kept giving everybody else fishy looks.

Our equipment manager, Bill Martell, started spraying deodorant around, but that didn't do any good. So one day after practice he took down one of the ceiling tiles where the smell seemed to be strongest. A big, dead rat fell out. It must have been there a couple of weeks. We all looked at each other and burst out laughing.

"It sure is nice to play in the big leagues, you go first class all the way," Doug said.

On the road they always put us up in some out-of-the-way place. When we went down to play Miami they had us way the hell out in Key Biscayne. When we played New York we stayed in Saddlebrook, New Jersey. Maybe they thought it was too far to drive to Toots Shor's and give the game plan away.

One year when we went out to play San Francisco they put us up in Oakland. It was above a fifteen-dollar cab ride to Frisco and there was no decent place to eat around the hotel. At the meeting that night Rick Evey, a defensive tackle who's now with Detroit, asked the Old Man why we were staying there.

The Old Man hit the table with his fist. "What the hell did we come out here to do, play the 49ers or eat at the Wharf?"

"We've always had bad luck staying in Frisco," the Old Man said. "The Packers stayed out here and beat them. Philly stayed out here and beat them, so did Detroit. All the American League teams stay here."

"That's why we're staying here. We're changing things a little bit. So quit worrying about where you're staying and start thinking about the game tomorrow."

After the meeting some of the guys ran over to the manager and asked him if the other teams stayed there.

"No," he said. "We thought it was a mistake when the Bears called and said they wanted reservations."

We asked him about the other American League teams.

"Well they stay here because their stadium is right across the street."

It turned out to be a cheap shack-up joint. The walls were so thin I could hear people walking down the hallway. About midnight I heard a couple of guys and broads in the next room giggling and laughing. I knelt up in bed and put my ear to the wall. They were making a lot of noise and I heard them call one girl Jane.

I got out of bed and tiptoed down the hall and got their room number. I came back in and called their room. A guy answered.

"Hello."

"Hello, is Jane there?"

"Jane? No, there's no Jane here."

"C'mon, I know Jane's in there. I saw you come in."

"No, there's no Jane here. You must have the wrong number."

"Well, maybe I do, but could you keep the noise down in there?"

I hung up and ran to the wall.

"He asked for you Jane. How did he know you were here?"

"I don't know. No one knew I was coming."

I kept my ear to the wall and pretty soon they started laughing it up again. By now my roommate, Joe Fortunato, was awake. He was giving me a funny look as he watched me kneeling in bed with my ear to the wall.

I motioned him over and he started listening. I told him to stay there while I phoned the room again. This time a girl answered.

"Listen, I know Jane's in there. I want to talk to her or else I'm going to have to call the manager."

"No, there's no Jane here. You must have the wrong number." Then she hung up.

I ran back to the wall.

"Jane, they know you're in here." She sounded like she was almost in tears.

I thought for sure they were going to hear Joe giggling.

One of them asked, "Do you think we ought to call the manager and trace the call?"

Then the other guy said, "I think we better go. Let's get the hell out of here."

They ran out the door while Joe and I rolled on the beds laughing like hell.

What the hell are we doing here anyway? What's the sense of going out today? We've got one more game left and it doesn't mean a goddamn thing to either team. Minnesota will try to score just one touchdown and then run the ball a hundred times and try to win 7–0, or 7–3, or 7–6.

They've already said their first two quarterbacks, Gary Cuozzo and Norm Snead, aren't going to play. They're going to play Buddy Lee or Bobby Lee or whatever the hell his name is. Gene Washington's not going to play. Their first-string backfield's not going to play. They're saving everybody for the playoffs, so what the hell are we going out for?

The park district finally rigged up some kind of lights so we could see something and I asked Doug and Randy Jackson for their explanations of why we're going out, if they knew a single reason why we should go out. "Yeah, because Abe came in and said we're going out." I said, "Hey, what the hell, that's a great reason."

Then O'B came walking in and that perked me up. I don't know if what he was doing you could really call walking. I suppose you could. He was all doubled over. He took a couple of real hard shots in the ribs at Green Bay and his neck was screwed up some way too. He was twisted up like the root of a tree.

That's courage. This guy is all busted up and here he comes ready to go out and do it all over again. If you get nothing else out of this game you learn to respect a man for his courage because you know what it takes.

That's what this game is all about, I guess. That's what a team is all about, the sacrifices one guy makes for another. That's the kind of thing that brings a team closer together.

I knew it was bothering him, that it hurt like hell, but it was just cracking me up to look at him, all twisted and hunched over like that. And at the same time I couldn't help liking him just that much more.

Percival, who's now the player rep, called a meeting to explain the new life insurance policy. We get an extra $10,000 coverage paid out of our annual dues. Somebody must have a friend in the life insurance business.

When he got through with that he passed out the ballots for the annual Whizzer White Award given to the most outstanding player-citizen. It's made at the annual players' association dinner. Then Mac distributed the ballots for the players' association all-pro team.

The meeting was kind of dragging along and Ed was pissed and uncomfortable and he started hollering, "Let's get this goddamn show on the road. Let's get this meeting over with and let's get the hell out of here." One thing about Ed, he never hides them or keeps his feelings to himself.

59

As soon as it ended I grabbed Spot Moore and Fig Newton and told them to start collecting money for the team's gift to O'B on his day. I tried to get everyone to give ten dollars but the team only voted a lousy five dollars. I wanted to get a bond and put it in his kids' names. Then Moore told me the black players decided they weren't going to give anything because O'B doesn't like blacks and never did.

That really pissed me off. I felt like just chucking the whole thing, or just puking. It disgusted me. We're all supposed to be a team. No wonder we're losers. Just a couple of days ago these guys who won't give now were all at Concannon's party and grabbing every prize that came their way with both hands. They didn't say anything about that. But now when they're asked to give a lousy five dollars as part of a team gift for a guy who's been around ten years they call him a racist. What the hell does that make them? I felt the least we could do is give O'B a little recognition for his years on the team. Ed, Bobby Joe and Jim Cadile are the only survivors of the 1963 squad Bears' last championship team. Ed was one of the heroes. He intercepted a pass off Y. A. Tittle to set up the winning touchdown.

Maybe that's the way Ed feels and maybe it's not. Maybe it just looks like that to the black guys. He's been around for a long time now and most of them have only been with the Bears for a few years. It's a new type of society and it's a new type of game now. Ed doesn't hardly talk to anyone, black or white.

Hell, most of the black guys don't talk to a lot of the white guys, and most of the black guys don't talk to each other. We've had black guys on the team who never associated with any other black players. You find that on every team. Throwing forty or fifty strangers together involves some pretty complicated personal relationships. There aren't too many guys I talk to.

Some guys just hit it off better than others no matter what color they are. It's a matter of personality. We've had a couple of guys, white guys, whose only associations on the team were with black guys. A lot could come into it—if we were winning—if the season was just starting—who knows?

But we've never had any race problems on the Bears, not that

I've been aware of anyway. That's why this thing comes as such a shock to me. Whenever anyone thinks he's getting a bad deal we get it right out in the open and try to clear it up. Or at least we try to. Maybe they withhold stuff at the meetings too. You never know.

A couple of years ago the players got together before the season and really let their hair down. It lasted a couple of hours, and anything that anybody had to say got said. One guy tried to blame all his troubles on being black, but even the black guys were telling him they weren't going to let him hide behind his blackness.

If any of the black guys have a bitch they go to George Seals, Willie Holman, and Bennie McRae, when he was here, and talk it over. If it sounds legitimate they can take it to Paul Patterson and then to Muggs or the Old Man. Patterson is director of player relations. His job is to work with the black players, take care of any problems they might have, line them up with jobs, help them any way he can. That's not copping a plea for the organization. They'd be stupid if they didn't do it.

When I first met Seals I thought he was awfully touchy, very temperamental about black and white. I thought he was a racist. But after I got to know him, played with him a few years, I really got to like him. We kid around a lot, things like, he'll say, nothing much going on in the ghetto, or well, I gotta get back to the ghetto, when he's leaving the locker room.

Bennie McRae was our player representative before he was traded to New York. Then it was Seals, now it's Percival. These guys were elected because they deserved it and wanted it. There was no black-white bloc voting. No racist campaigning for the job. They got it because everybody thought they'd do a good job.

If you want a purely personal observation I think part of the problem is ego. It takes a helluva ego to play this game, or to be successful in any field. Anybody who plays regularly thinks he ought to be treated like a star, but for a lot of reasons that have nothing to do with race every regular doesn't get treated the same way. That's show biz. But it's also a good thing, because without that driving ego, everybody thinking he's the best at what he's doing, he wouldn't be worth a damn at all. Hell, I've seen guys make it on sheer ego, beat out guys who had much better physical tools.

You can't respect guys and be a racist at the same time, and who can't respect a Sayers or an Eller, or a Deacon Jones, or a Page, or a Bobby Bell. I've never seen any evidence of racism in any all-pro or pro bowl or All-Star voting of any kind.

For years Frank Robinson, a black man, was the leader of the Baltimore Orioles. They had plenty of white stars on those teams, but Robinson was the leader, the guy who pulled them together. Maury Wills with the Dodgers is another one.

St. Louis busted up their team. From what I hear it was mostly because of race problems. They're still trading guys. But one guy they never traded is Ernie McMillan. He's a helluva guy and a great player. My brother Ron knew him at Illinois. He and O'Bradovich were both offensive ends down there. Maybe the problem in St. Louis was as much with the management as it was with the players.

Look at Dallas and Duane Thomas. At least he played there. He lasted about three days with New England. At Kansas City about half the team is black. Hank Stram has a reputation for getting along well with blacks, but he had trouble with Mike Garrett. Who knows what that was about. Everybody seems to like Weeb Ewbank. Nobody ever complains about having to play in New York.

Big cities like New York and Chicago are in a different situation compared to teams in smaller cities like Green Bay and Denver. In places like that you can get a hundred percent participation in team social functions simply because everybody lives closer together. In Chicago everybody's all spread out in different directions. I know, I live about seventy-five miles away from some of the other guys.

But one thing's for sure. If there is a team function or an invitation to the team we're all invited or nobody goes. I know one guy called Abe and said he wanted to have a party for the team and then started hinting around that he didn't want any of the blacks. Abe told him to go to hell.

You get guys from all parts of the country, from all kinds of different social structures and backgrounds. You get whites who never associated with blacks and blacks who never associated with whites. Living in Chicago I've known blacks all my life. There has always been free and easy access, no matter what anyone says.

On the field everybody's the same color to me. There's no nigger or whitey out there. Everybody looks alike to me. If they wear that other jersey I hate them all equally. I either knock them down or they knock me down. I don't look to see what color a man is before I hit him. That's why this stuff with Ed surprised and hurt me.

We're supposed to be a team. You play with these guys and that means you have to sacrifice yourself for the good of the team. You give your best to win. You try to throw that extra block or make that extra play that will help you win. You sacrifice yourself so that maybe someone else can make the big play, and then they pull this crap.

Then we had to sit there and watch that Green Bay game. Abe gave everybody hell. Everybody was just plain horseshit. I saw where I got knocked out. It was a running play with Brockington. We were gang tackling him and I tried to get under everybody and caught a knee in the head for my trouble. I saw all kinds of things I didn't remember. It was like watching a game I didn't play in.

After the Green Bay film Abe passed out some more all-pro ballots. They were really ballots for the all-conference team. We were only supposed to pick guys in the NFC, and you couldn't vote for anyone on your own team.

Everyone nominated whomever they felt like, and you just put whomever you wanted down on your own ballot. We just voted for the offensive guys and our offense picked the defensive team.

I put Roger Staubach of the Cowboys down at quarterback, not so much for what he did against us, but for what he did after they played us. I voted for an awful lot of Packers it seems. I put down Ken Bowman at center. He's steady, and he's always played well against us. At the guards the guys who got the votes were Gale Gillingham of the Packers, Tom Mack of the Rams, and John Niland of the Cowboys.

63

Rayfield Wright of Dallas was the only tackle I voted for. The other guys were voting for Rocky Freitas of the Lions and Cas Banaszek of the 49ers. At tight end the nominations were for Charlie Sanders of the Lions and Ted Kwalick of the 49ers. I think just about everybody picked Sanders.

The running backs were John Brockington and Donny Anderson of the Packers, Steve Owens of the Lions and Duane Thomas of the Cowboys. I thought Brockington was the best back we played all year. Larry Csonka and Jim Kiick are both good backs, but they're not in our conference. Thomas didn't show us anything. Along with Brockington I took Anderson. The guy's a helluva player. He can run, pass, block, and kick. What else is there?

For the wide receivers they were voting for Bob Hayes of the Cowboys, Roy Jefferson of the Redskins, Carroll Dale of the Packers, Lance Rentzel of the Rams and Gene Washington of the 49ers. I didn't vote for any wide receivers. I didn't think I came in contact with any of them enough to tell who was really better. Why should I vote for a guy just because he can run fast or he has a big reputation.

When we broke up the meeting I told Ed what had happened. Maybe I shouldn't have, but I was so goddamned mad and disgusted I couldn't keep it to myself. I knew if I told anyone else they'd just shrug their shoulders as if to say, so, what else is new? Part of the reason I told him I suppose is just that I wanted to disassociate myself from those bastards. I didn't want him to think that I was part of them. I wanted him to know that I thought more of him than that.

He just looked at me and shook his head and said, "Aw shit, I've had it. I've just had it." And he walked out. Ed just walked out, got in his car and drove off. I wish the hell I would have gone with him.

We hit the field, did a lap around the goal posts, and Abe started talking about how Minnesota has blocked a couple of kicks this year, and how we've got to be up and alert. And I'm standing there in the damn cold, damp mist and this guy—we're in our fourteenth week now, plus six exhibitions, that's twenty weeks—is still going over the same crap out there and we still make the same mistakes week after week, and it's the same guys making them.

Now he says he wants to beef up the punting team. He wants Doug up on a wing and he wants me at fullback to protect Bobby Joe. I'm standing there and I look around at all the special teams and I see we have nothing but defensive players on them. There are hardly any offensive players on them anymore.

You'd think if you were going to try to stop someone from blocking a punt you'd use offensive players. They're supposed to be blockers aren't they? That's supposedly what they get paid for. Maybe that's just on other teams, not the Bears.

But no, Abe says he can't trust anybody else, so now he's got the whole defensive team in there. It isn't enough we're on the field the whole damn game because the offense can't move the ball, we still have to go down on the specialty teams.

I don't think there's another team in football that has to play so many regulars on the special teams. We've got guys, five starters, who are playing out their options. And we've got guys sitting on the bench who couldn't make my college team. They can't even trust these guys to go down under a kickoff or a punt or block for a lousy two-count. Why the hell don't they get rid of them and give the money they pay them to the guys who are earning it? I should have gone with O'B.

Hell, some guys have even refused to play on the special teams. Steve Wright said they told him to take a position on the kickoff blocking wedge and he told them, "Hey, wait a minute, you want an offensive tackle or a special team guy? Take your choice. You can't have both."

That's really a different attitude. I could never bring myself to do it no matter how much I wanted to. I love being on the field. I'd play offense if they'd let me. I'd never come off if I really had my way. What gets me though is having so many useless guys around while a few do all the work. Every Sunday it's like about fifteen or twenty of us against the other teams' forty. They just have to grind you down.

But Wright says he just wants to be an offensive tackle and doesn't want any part of those special teams. He said that something could happen that would put you out forever. He claimed he hurt his knee playing on the special teams when he was with the Packers and he'd never play on them again.

Wright's the guy who used to drive Lombardi to distraction. Lombardi would fly into almost uncontrollable rages at the guy. One day he lost control completely and started pounding Wright with his fists and screaming at him right on the practice field.

Steve just laughed at him. That's the kind of guy he is. In his own way he's as stubborn and determined as Lombardi. He's made up his mind that no one is going to make him do something he doesn't want to do. He's going to lead his life the way he wants to and no one is going to change him.

But what really gets me, what I really can't understand, is why they can't find eleven guys during the training camp and throughout the exhibition season to run down under a kickoff. And why can't some of these guys get it into their heads that by showing something on the kicking teams they can make the team? You'd think they'd bust their asses. I know I would.

After we finally got through standing around in the mist listening to Abe go over the kicking teams we went back into the locker for lunch, compliments of Earl Thomas and Jerry Moore.

Abe knows more people than a ward committeeman and he started a deal where a friend of his would bring in three big containers of hot Italian beef and sausage sandwiches and some beer and bottle or two of wine. The food was paid for out of the fines for screwing up on the kicking teams.

Thomas screwed up on a punt in the Denver game. He came out on the field and then thought we had twelve men on the field so he ran off. But he ran off on the Denver side, and that got us a penalty. It cost him a hundred-dollar fine.

Spot Moore screwed up in the Redskin game. He went dashing out to try and block a first quarter field goal. The only problem was that we already had eleven men out there trying it already. That cost us five yards, even though Curt Knight missed from the forty-four.

The penalty gave the Skins a first down on the thirty-two. We held them again, but this time Knight was good from the thirty.

At half time Abe said, "If we lose you can all blame Jerry Moore." That's what you call a real inspirational pep talk.

After practice Jay McGreevy took me to his place. We went

back into the vault, as he calls it. It's an old back room where his father stored a lot of wine. We pulled out a couple of old bottles we thought looked pretty good, and just to make sure Jay called some guy he knows who's supposed to be some sort of wine expert and asked him about them. He told us to go ahead and enjoy them, so we did.

We enjoyed them a little too much. I was late getting home. I was supposed to pick up Big Matt at my mother's because Helen had to take Nikki to dancing class. When I got there Helen was already there, and she wasn't too happy. I played with Matt for a while after we got home and looked at Nikki's school schedule. That didn't improve my frame of mind. I thought she was off until January tenth, and now I see she has to be back on the third.

Helen seemed cooled down enough so I told her that if I didn't go to the Pro Bowl I didn't want to come back from Florida until the end of January. Nikki missing a couple of weeks of school isn't going to hurt. If I have to go to the Pro Bowl we'll come home earlier, about the middle of January.

I took Matt and played with him for a while. I couldn't help laughing when I thought of Matt in the back of the camper for a couple of days. He's at that age now, almost a year, where he gets into everything. I thought, jeez, I'm going to be up front driving all the way to Florida and he's going to be like a wild Indian back there. It should be a good time for Helen. If she's mad now wait till we get to Lookout Mountain.

The lady from "Toys for Tots" called today. I'm supposed to be the Chicago area chairman. It's a group that collects toys and gifts for needy kids at Christmas time. I'd really like to help, because I really like kids. Maybe it's just adults I don't like. But my job is really just to have a couple of promotional pictures taken with some kids. That's not much to do for a chairman.

She wants me to go to Ford City Shopping Center one day this week for another picture. I'm going to have to make some time to go there. I've got a lot of running around to do. I have to pick up some tires, pick up the camper, drop off my car, start filling the camper with water and all the necessities, and make a check list, have the sway bars installed and then there's the defensive party and that kills Thursday all by itself.

We're talking about eating in Helen's in Blue Island. That's a Lithuanian place. Great food there. That's got to go down as one of my favorite spots along with John's Pizzeria in Calumet City and the Bull and Bush in Los Angeles. They all have great food.

Now I better work on my knee. Maybe I'd feel better if my knee was better. I have only about ninety degrees of flexion in it instead of the normal hundred and twenty or thirty. They tightened it up so much that I can't go full squat. We thought it would get stretched out through exercise, but it hasn't. They put me under once and broke it down, but we're afraid to try it again because if it swelled up or something I'd have to miss a game or two.

I'm doing the best I can, but I know it's not the best I can do. It's like being out of shape, or tired, or even lazy. You can see everything coming. You know what to do, but you're just a little late getting there. That's what gets so damn frustrating. That, and everyone asking me and quizzing me, oh, have you slowed down? You look a little slow out there. You looked like you were limping. Does your leg hurt?

Hell, what the hell do they want me to do, lay out a year? They expect me to make every tackle no matter where the ball goes. I suppose that's a helluva compliment, but right now it's a helluva annoyance. I never could cover Bob Hayes on a fly pattern.

This is the most aggravating, frustrating year I've ever lived through. It's worse than last year because last year I knew the knee was gone and was just playing from week to week hoping to make it through the season. If it went out before the end, well, we knew it was coming and it wouldn't have been a surprise or a disappointment. But I thought the operation would restore the knee to top efficiency and that finally I'd be able to go all out.

But we ran into trouble and it was in the cast about twice as long as it should have been and it aches like a son of a gun now. I haven't run full out all year. I'm lucky if I can go three-quarter speed. I have to really be anticipating to get out to the sweeps on time.

At practice, well, I'm just out there. I only take part in the

68

drills I can. On pass defense I just try to get to my area any way I can make it. They know it, both my coaches and the opposition. What the hell, they see the films too. They can see I'm having trouble moving.

Early in the year it was still sore and practicing and playing on that damn Astroturf never gave it a chance to rest. I kept telling them about it. All the guys were bitching. Everybody was having problems with their kness and ankles because of the sudden stops you make on that damn stuff. There's no give to it. We asked them to practice on the real grass at the north end of Soldier Field, beyond the stands. But they just ignored us.

When all those artificial turfs came out everyone, doctors included, were saying that this would cut down on knee and ankle injuries because with the smaller cleats you couldn't get them caught like you could in the grass. Now there are a whole bunch of reports coming out that completely contradict the first reports.

Now they say that the fake fields cause more injuries than real grass. But what the hell, it's good for the owners. They don't have to cut it, water it, resod it, or maintain it in any way. No matter what the weather it shows up well on television. The announcers always know what yard line the ball is on. It's good for the fans because no one's number ever gets muddy. The only people who don't like it are the players, and hell, they're only around for a couple of years anyway, so why worry about them? They can always get new ones.

After a game it takes me two days just to be able to walk straight. That brings me to Wednesday before I can begin to take part in the practice. Now the cold weather is here and it's a bitch. The knee is stiff and aches, and Fox tells me that it's an arthritic condition I'm going to have to learn to live with. He said it was caused by all those years of the joint rubbing without sufficient protection.

That's why I like to play in warm weather. In Los Angeles it was hot and my knee loosened up. It felt real good in Miami too. But what good does it do to talk about it. Like Steve Wright said, they really make it miserable for you here. He's been with about four teams now, I guess he should know.

A lot of guys think they have to be pampered. They always say, "Well, you have to make the players feel good before you can get anything out of them." That may be right, part right, but I don't believe in spoiling them either.

I was talking to George Seals and he was telling me he was on some TV show earlier in the year and he met a dealer who wanted to give a color TV set to the offensive and defensive players of the week. They asked the Old Man if it was okay and he said no!

There is a lot of stuff that goes on but I try to ignore it. Either that or go crazy. I don't like to hear about it because then I'd have to start hating this whole organization and I don't want to. I don't hear too much because for the most part I'm a loner. I don't associate with many of the guys except maybe to have lunch or a beer after practice or go out to dinner on a road trip.

Some guys tell me, "Well you don't have anything to complain about, not for what you're getting paid." So I just agree with them. At practice they joke around and ask me if I was out the night before. I tell them, "How can I go out when I have to look at films and go over the game plan and the computer results that tell us how to beat everyone. You guys don't have to do that."

So they come back, "But we're not getting paid for that. You are."

That's beside the point. I could still play as well as I could and play just for myself without looking at all the movies and reading all that stuff. I do it for the whole team.

When you ask a guy with the Bears why he plays and what he gets out of playing you know there are reasons other than winning. You just go on your own personal pride. I never thought I could be that way, but I've learned painfully that you have to. I learned that you have to think of yourself first because no one is going to think of you at all.

It galls the hell out of me when I see the Old Man come out to practice and he sees the kind of practice that's going on. Nobody's even damp under the arms. He can see the kind of practice the head coach is running. He's been around for over fifty years so how in the hell can he help from seeing.

5

Wednesday, December 15

It's funny how nothing ever works out the way you imagine it.

I suppose most of the pleasures are in the anticipation. Then maybe if you really do accomplish something you can look back and say, well, I did it. That should give you an inner satisfaction.

I've always had that anticipation, all my life. I hope someday to be able to sit back and say, well, I did what I wanted to do. I'm satisfied.

That's how it was when I was selected for the College All-Star team. It was something I dreamed about since I was old enough to know what it meant. After I was picked though I didn't get the idea that I could say, well, I have it made, I was too worried about making the team. I didn't want to be just picked for the team. They pick about sixty. I wanted to be one of the eleven who play.

The All-Star game was a great honor for me. When I started playing it was a far-off star I aimed at reaching. Outside of my mother and father I don't think I ever let on to anyone just how much I wanted to make it. I looked forward to playing in that game for years, and because it originated in Chicago it seemed doubly important.

But at the same time I told myself that if I didn't make the team, or if I didn't play well in the game, it didn't matter because what really counted was how I did when I reported to the Bears.

I began to think that the three weeks I spent in the All-Star camp might hurt me in trying to make the Bears. I kept telling myself that it could be beneficial. This would be the first time that I'd come up against the pros, and I'd be playing the best, the world champion Cleveland Browns. I expected to learn pro techniques from the All-Star coaching staff and it worked out that way. I learned a lot about pass defense, or rather I started to learn.

No college team can throw the ball like the pros. They don't have the passers. They don't have the receivers. They don't mask their plays like the pros. They don't have the finesse to run the screens and draws the way the pros do.

We learned from some smart football men. Otto Graham was our head coach and Johnny Sauer was his head defensive assistant. Sauer spent a lot of time with us. They tried to run us hard and run a no-nonsense camp. I stayed after regular practice almost every day with the other two linebackers, Marty Schottenheimer and Don Croftchek. We'd work on getting back into our zones as quickly as possible and learn to read screens and draws and work on our red dogs.

Marty and I met at an All-Star game in Buffalo about a month earlier. He told me later that when he first met me he thought I was a big hot dog from all the ink I was getting in my senior year. He said nobody could be that good. With newspapers and magazines you're either Superman or Humpty Dumpty. There's nothing in the middle, except ninety percent of the players. I had a pretty good night at Buffalo and that seemed to break the ice.

The three of us worked hard, but I was disappointed in a lot of the others. Not too many of them had what I thought was a good attitude toward the game with the Browns. They thought they were there for a party. They'd go to the Playboy Club at night and act like prima donnas on the field. Hell, I was from Chicago, but I never left camp to go home or go night clubbing downtown.

The two leagues were still fighting their war for talent and some of these guys made a lot of money. They thought they had it made. There were some I thought didn't belong there at all. You read a lot about other guys and you come to regard them as something really special, as being on a higher plateau. You tend to believe everything you read unless you've had some prior contact. You're awed by reputation. I never thought of myself as having any reputation, and certainly not a hot dog, the impression Marty had. After a couple of days of scrimmaging I didn't think anyone was really special. Actually I was let down a little.

We had some good times, free and easy times, especially for about sixty strangers who are suddenly thrown in together. Everybody kidded around about how much money some of the guys signed for. Ralph Neely was famous. Everybody kidded him about getting a ranch and some oil wells. Neely signed with both Houston and the Cowboys and it had to get straightened out in court. They kidded me about signing a lifetime contract with the Old Man. There was really more talk about money than there was about football.

About a week before the game they took us down to Rensselaer to scrimmage the Bears. It wasn't a game, just a controlled scrimmage. There were no kickoffs, and each team would start at the twenty and run ten plays. Coming up against a pro team was something I had been anticipating for a long time now, and the first one I faced was the one I was going to be with.

We all thought of the Bears as something special. They won the championship the year before the Browns and they had the reputation of being a rough, very physical team. They all looked so big, guys like Doug Atkins and Earl Leggett and Mike Ditka. When some of the guys got their first look at them they started oohing and aahing.

They came out hard and tough. They were really chopping us down, blocking real low, and tying us up with crab blocks. Everything they ran was quick and snappy—boom, boom, boom. I was really impressed in the first half, but then as we went along I found I could stay on the field with them and some of that awe wore off. In the second half we did a pretty good job with them.

There were a couple of mix-ups, tempers got a little hot and feelings a bit high, but there were no actual fights. One series they were down close to our goal line and they sent the fullback, Joe Marconi, off tackle. He didn't make it, but they thought he did, and started bitching at the officials. I don't know if they were trying to impress us or not, but they kept bitching at the officials all day. That's one difference between the colleges and pros, in the colleges you hardly say a word to the officials, and then it's just yes sir, and no sir.

73

Finally after all those years of looking forward to that game I had the double honor of being elected one of the captains. Our quarterback, Roger Staubach, was elected offensive captain, and I was the defensive captain. That honor was a little dampened though when I got slightly middled in a little controversy.

It was over Gale Sayers. Gale said he was hurt and wasn't taking much part in the drills.

I don't know if Sayers got hurt in the Bears scrimmage or before. Graham said he couldn't find out what was bothering him, and he made a few statements about Gale not having the guts to make it in pro ball.

Graham is a pretty intense guy and very outspoken. He's the kind of person who wants an instant response, and is very impatient if he doesn't get one. We were at dinner a couple of nights before the game and Graham came over and told me he was on the verge of cutting Sayers from the team. He said that Sayers didn't want to do anything, that he was loafing.

I didn't know what to say. What could I tell him? He was the coach. But I didn't know what was behind it. I didn't know Gale's reasons. Maybe the Bears told him to take it easy if he was hurt. I doubt if anyone, even the Bears, knew or had any idea that Sayers was going to turn out as great as he did. All I knew was that they didn't say anything to me about taking it easy.

I told Graham I'd help him if I could, but that I didn't see what I could do. Gale's a quiet guy, and when he doesn't want to talk, he doesn't talk. So Graham said he'd let me know, but he just let the thing slide. I think a few people talked to him and cooled him down, but I don't think he played Gale that night.

Game night was hot and muggy and raining, a typical early August Friday night in Chicago. I was worried about one thing. I know this sounds silly, but I was worried about whether or not they were going to introduce us.

Every All-Star game I've ever been in, when they introduce a hometown boy he always gets a big hand. I worked and waited eight years to get into that game. I had been looking forward to running under those goal posts and up that field since I was a kid in grammar school. So many nights I pictured myself, my

74

name being called over the loudspeaker, and the cheers. But here was the rain.

They went ahead and introduced us anyway. It was great. I got my kicks. It felt real good, just the way I'd imagined it.

Cleveland had a good team, and my job was mostly to key on and go after Jim Brown. They liked to run him on sweeps and off-tackle cutbacks and throw him those little swing passes. Everytime I watched him on TV I'd see guys bump into him and make half-assed attempts to tackle him. It looked like they were afraid of him. Then everyone would say, gee, he's a helluva runner.

I just concentrated on tackling him, getting my head and shoulder into him and not trying to make one-armed passes at him. I don't think he broke away from me.

I'm not trying to take anything away from Brown. How could I with the record he made for himself? He was a great runner. He had size, speed, and he was smart. He knew how to pace himself and get everything he could out of his blockers. When he was in the open and had to run over someone he could do that too. He was also a fine pass receiver. As a matter of fact, after seven years, he's still the best runner I ever faced.

What I am saying though is that he seemed to have an awful lot of guys intimidated. Well, if he did, more power to him. That's part of football too.

We were at a banquet once and I was sitting next to Brown and he started telling me how he made Sam Huff.

Brown said that whenever Cleveland played New York the papers always built the game up as a personal duel between him and Huff. Brown said that if it hadn't been for him no one would have ever heard of Sam Huff.

Lennie Moore was there with Brown and he just agreed with everything Brown said, as if he were some kind of oracle. That's right, Jimmy, that's right.

The Browns beat us, but we tried not to make it too easy for them, although Frank Ryan was able to throw against our secondary. He overthrew Paul Warfield on one bomb and Warfield broke his shoulder or collar bone trying to make a diving catch.

I don't even remember the score. I was in a hurry to drive to camp in Rensselaer the next morning. It's what I had really been waiting for all my life.

George Allen worked me right into the defensive practices. The Bears used a lot of red dogs then, but the main thing I had to learn was their terminology. They used a combination number and key-word system. All teams use similar systems, but everyone uses different names for the same things.

Allen was a great explainer, and he'd review my responsibilities right on the field. He'd be talking about "skin" and "sky" and I'd listen very intently with only the vaguest idea of what he was talking about.

There were so many new names and terms to remember at first that they were easy to confuse. They were all related and most were alliterative. That added to my confusion for a day or so.

For instance, "skin" and "sky" are keys the linebackers use on pass coverage. A back going outside the end for a pass was a "sky." He's the responsibility of the outside linebacker. If the back comes inside the end it was a "skin," and the middle linebacker has to take him. Interpreting the key words in terms of my responsibilities on the play took a little getting used to.

Allen's meetings were different than any others that I've had to sit through. He'd come in with a clipboard and go over the mistake that everyone made that day. He'd correct them and then, explain exactly what he wanted done. This meeting was over as soon as he finished the list. He never rambled or went off on tangents the way some coaches do.

Allen substituted a lot during practice. He gave everyone a shot. All coaches don't do that either. Some of them let one man play the whole defensive period and just let the others stand around as dummies during the offensive drills.

I wasn't the only middle linebacker in camp. Bill George was there. He practically invented the position. George used to be a middle guard, but one day he got up out of his four-point stance, took a step backward, and became a middle linebacker.

That was also the birth of the four-three defense that is now the standard pro defense. Clark Shaughnessy, the father of the modern T formation, said that George was the smartest man who ever played the game. He built the Bears defense around George.

O'Bradovich said there was never anybody like him. He said George could look at the quarterback or the formation and know exactly where the play was going, and he'd do it time after time, not just once in a while. He said George would holler to the front four and tell them when the play was coming at them.

Mike Reilly was there too. He got there the year before. He acted very buddy-buddy with George, called him "Greek" as if he were his partner before Larry Morris, Fortunato, and Atkins.

In the exhibition games Reilly played the first and third quarters and I'd play the second and fourth. George was hurt. He had a hamstring pull and he was just comig off a knee operation so he didn't play at all.

A day or two after every game we'd review the movies. Whenever Reilly would make a tackle George would holler, "Great tackle Mike. Geez, run that back."

Dave Whitsell was the same way. "Look at me on this play," he'd shout. "Look at that tackle I made. Run that again."

Look at me do this. Look at me do that. Look at me. I couldn't believe how they joked around in the film sessions. In college when we were reviewing the films we sat there with our mouths shut. If the coaches wanted to bring something up, okay. But we didn't dare say, hey, look at how great I am. Look at me. Run that back.

When I was on the screen they wouldn't say anything when I did something right. If I made a tackle they were quiet. But if I made a mistake and Allen let it go by George or Reilly would say, "Well coach, isn't Mac (that's the name we use for the middle linebacker) supposed to take that man?" Or, "Isn't Mac supposed to go the other way?"

And Allen would say, "Oh yeah Dick, you made a mistake. You should have gone the other way," or correct whatever it was I did wrong.

But George and Reilly never called attention to the mistakes Reilly made. He didn't make a lot of mistakes. He was a good player.

I was really naïve then. It never dawned on me that this was some sort of rookie hazing. I was too big to wear a beanie. After all, I was a rookie and didn't know how they did things in the big leagues. I didn't realize it was part of my indoctrination.

At first I resented it though, and who do you think was my roommate on the road, Reilly. I got to know him a little better and found out he's a good guy. I was sorry to see him go when he was traded to the Vikings a couple of years ago.

But all the players knew what was going on. It was a secret joke. I finally got let in on it after the Baltimore game about halfway through the season. We beat them pretty good, shut them out in fact, and we were having a little dinner party after the game and some of the guys started laughing about what Mike and Bill were doing during the movie sessions.

I hardly saw the Old Man that year. He was the head coach, but I hardly saw him. From what I could see he just rode around the field in his golf cart checking up on his assistants. He supervised them while they supervised us. He spent most of his time with the offense. He was the one calling the shots, there was no mistaking that. He set the rules and he enforced them.

I couldn't wait to get to my first training camp. I thought they were going to open the top of my head and pour in all this knowledge. That's where you'll get it all I'd tell myself. That's where they teach you their style.

The only thing I got was trial and error, just like high school and just like college. Whatever I learned I learned for myself, the hard way. I think I learned more from Bill George in the short time he was with us until he went to the Rams. They were little things, pointers, tips, keys and clues to different players and different formations and systems, but over the season they added up to a helluva lot of information that man passed on to me, and I was the one who took his job away from him.

Now all that anticipation is over and you kind of get blasé. Everything takes on a repetitiveness—Monday off; Tuesday, game films; Wednesday, first half of the game plan; Thursday, the second half of the game plan; Friday, review; Saturday, short review. Sunday is game day and it starts all over again.

These are places I've been before. Let's see, seven years times twenty games a year that's one hundred and forty, plus Pro Bowl games. It gets to be a job just as much as going to the office or the shop is a job for everybody else. The glamour must be in someone else's mind. It's sure not in mine.

Just like every other craftsman I have to keep my tools in good repair so I go to see Bernie. I've been scared since the first part of the year when I did all those stretching exercises before the Steeler game and then I couldn't even walk on it. So now, if anything, I've become more conscious of it.

Bernie rubs it down real good and bends it back. He said he thought it was bending a lot further than before. It really felt good in the weight room. I seemed to be getting a little more flexion and movement than at any time in the last five weeks. I was able to put some really heavy pressure on it. Here we are coming up to the last game and I'm just starting to get in shape.

I felt good when I got into the team meeting, like I was raring to go. Abe was taking his time, going over the Vikings real slow. That's not like Abe. He's usually a kind of fast-talking, bang, bang, bang guy. He said that Lee was going to be the Vikings quarterback. I don't know how he found out so early in the week, but these coaches must have some sort of spy system or grapevine all their own.

I know George Allen must. He must have some way of getting our defensive game plan, or else he's a great mind reader. The Redskins seemed to know exactly what we were going to be doing all the time. Everytime we rotated our deep backs to the wide side of the field they'd run to the short side.

Now if the strong safety doesn't play run first we're in trouble. If he takes a step or two back they isolate the outside linebacker. It's like he's on an island. He has to cover both the inside and the outside. They can run anywhere they want. There's no one there to force the play back into the pursuit or wide into the sideline. The Redskins had a lot of success with that against us.

Abe passed out the game plan for the Vikings, and we went over it together. It's for normal situations what we do on first and ten; second and plus seven; second and minus seven; and all the plays the Vikings run in those situations. There aren't too many. The Vikings believe in keeping it simple.

We go over their different formations: when they split their backs; strong right and strong left; the different ways the backs

79

line up; how they use their wide receivers; and what they run from the different formations.

I try to pay close attention because I'm the one who's going to have to recognize these keys during the game. I'm the one who has to call our defenses. I'll take it all home with me tonight with some Vikings' game films and spend time on it. We're putting in some new red dogs so I'll diagram them for myself and draw in each player's assignment. I'll keep going through it until it's firm in my mind—the situation in which to call the dogs and each man's responsibility.

Then I break down their tendencies; if they run to the strong side of the formation which hole do they like to run to? How many times? How many times and where do they run from each formation? When do they run to the strong side? When do they run to the weak side? When do they like to run their screens and draws?

That'll keep me busy for an hour or so tonight. If it was a team like Dallas that uses a lot of different formations and motion I'd have to spend more time, but Minnesota gives you a pretty simple set most of the time.

Everybody gets one, but maybe all the guys don't look at their game plans at night. Maybe it's not important for them to know what the calls will be and why, other than knowing their own assignments.

Maybe just going through it at practice is enough. I doubt it though. I can't see how knowing what kind of plays the opposition likes to run is going to hurt no matter what position you play. There's a chance it may even help.

Allen and Fortunato were very big on studying the other team's tendencies. They used the computer to tell them what different teams did in different situations. It really helps in a lot of cases because most teams don't change very much from year to year. But what people tend to forget is that what they do against four other teams isn't necessarily what they're going to do against you. In a lot of cases what a team will try or won't try depends on how the different personnel match up.

When we were preparing for the 49ers a couple of years ago the coaches kept telling us they liked to run a late trap—a draw play with trap blocking. They used it all season long against

*Dick, at twenty-one months,
with brother Dave's
homemade scooter*

*Dick and Helen
in high school*

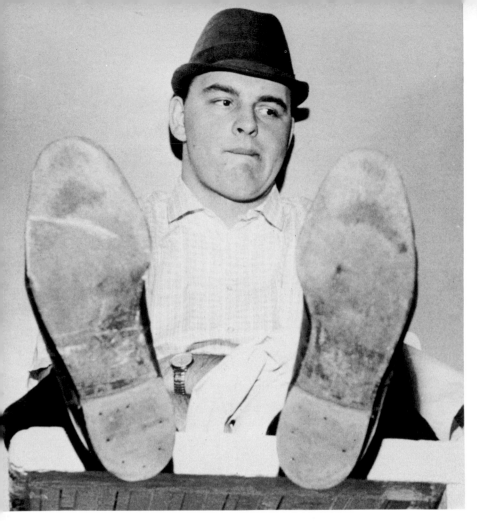

A sophomore in high school

Butkus during his sophomore year at the
University of Illinois–UPI

Prep football player of the year–AP

With Coach Pete Elliott
after beating Washington in the Rose Bowl–AP

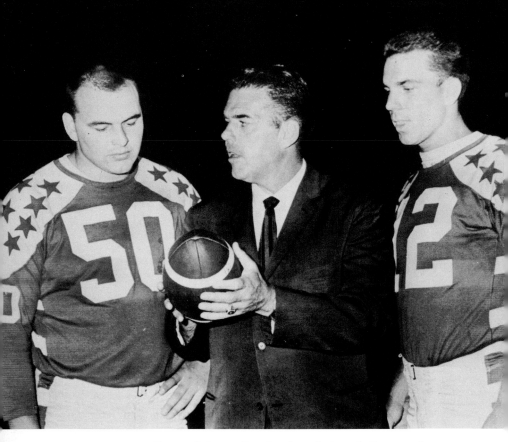

Captains Butkus and Roger Staubach with Coach Otto Graham before the College All-Star game–AP

With Bears' defensive coach, George Allen

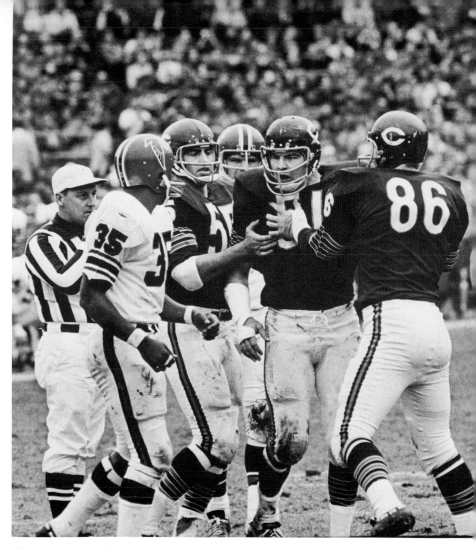

"Sir, I not only disagree with what you say,
but question your right to say it."

Just before the snap

Waiting to get back into the game against the Redskins, September 1968

What it's all about

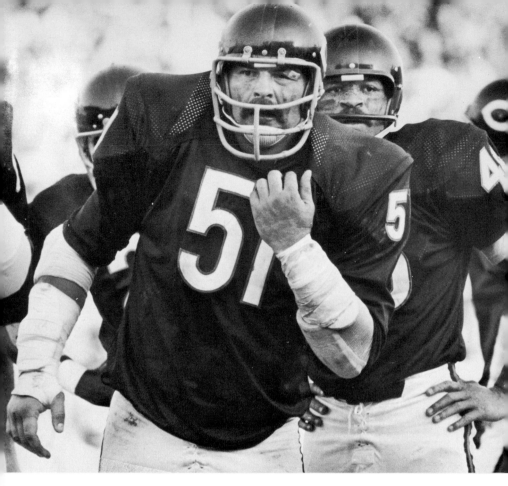

The middle linebacker

A break between plays

After the Viking Game

The catch that won the game against the Redskins

Dick, Helen, Nikki, and Ricky

every one of their opponents. We worked on it all week; what situations they liked to run it in and what formations they ran it out of. So they didn't run it once against us. They ran some lates, but no late traps.

You have to take your own personnel into consideration in making up any game plan. Maybe they didn't have to trap us. A trap block works well against a quick penetrating front four. Then the main thing is taking out the middle linebacker. But maybe they figured they could handle our tackles with regular blocking. Then they get the center to occupy me and have the back read which way I react and then bust off the opposite way.

Now this year when we played the 49ers they used the late trap against us. They kept using it right along against everyone, but all week long getting ready for that game I was remembering what happened in the past. So in my own mind I had to get ready for both possibilities.

For the Miami game our scouting report said that when they were in a Black formation, that's with the left back on the side of the tight end and the fullback behind the quarterback, it's the halfback who carries the ball. The first time they came out in that formation I went with the tip and sent the line to the left. So they sent Csonka to the right, the fullback to the right, a complete opposite of our scouting report. I knew then it was going to be a long night.

My calls are basically for the rush defense. I call everybody's rush route. It's just a number, or a key word: Forty-Six Tight, or Jet-Eye. The first number, Four, puts them in an even four-man line. If the first number was a Five that'd be for an odd-man line. One of the tackles would line up over the center. The second number, Six, and the key, Tight, tells them what route to take. I'm not necessarily anticipating where they're going to run.

If I call a Tight, or Wide, that refers to the way the tackles are supposed to rush. On a Tight they both pinch in toward the center to clog up the middle. On a Wide their charge is to the guards' outside shoulders. That makes me responsible for everything up the middle. If I tell them Weak or Strong that means I want them to slant their charge toward the strong or weak side of the formation.

I never key on any one man. I don't think you can, unless he's a Jim Brown or a Sayers who you know is going to carry the ball twenty to thirty times a game. If you do, all they have to do is use him as a decoy and you take yourself right out of the play.

If we're hot it's easy to make the calls. I make them quick and we get right in and out of the huddle. If a team is driving on us and making good yardage and keeping us off balance I call a couple of red dogs to get the guys going instead of laying back and letting them pound-pound us.

The real problem calls are the third-down red dogs, our maximum red dogs and safety blitzes. A lot depends on the other team's formations. In the past against Dallas we had so many goofy calls to make just to keep up with all their formations that it hurt us a lot of times.

Outside of the red dogs the toughest situations are third and medium, like three or four yards. Most teams are mixing their plays often enough so you don't know if they will either run or pass on those downs. In this way they force the defense to play it honest.

In passing situations the deep backs and linebackers have to coordinate their coverage with the pass rush. If you're going to blitz on third and long you have to mask it well enough so they don't know it's coming. And you have to make sure you don't leave anybody wide open whom the quarterback can dump the ball to.

Now everyone is using the zone. But it still comes down to personnel no matter what systems or formations you use. Great pass rushers like Carl Eller and Alan Page can make any secondary look good. You just can't give the quarterback twenty seconds to throw the damn ball.

At the full team meeting this morning Dooley was saying that we need a maximum defensive effort. "Just hold them to seventeen points defense. Get us that ball and we'll win Sunday." He's been saying that a lot this season. Sometimes it works, but hell, we held Denver to six points and still lost. Who the hell can you beat when your offense scores two touchdowns in five games?

The first time I remember him saying that was his first season as head coach. We were going out to play the Rams. There were

82

only two games left in the season, and the Rams, I think, were still undefeated. If we could win our last two games we still had a shot at the division title.

All week long Dooley kept preaching, just hold them under seventeen points and we'll win. Hold them defense. He kept saying it over and over, but I wonder if anyone really believed him. We were all crippled up. Sayers was out for the season. Concannon fractured his collarbone earlier and a hard tackle might put him out.

That didn't leave much in the way of offense, and anyone analyzing the personnel of the two teams would have to go with the Rams as easy winners. But just as you can't always rely on the scouting reports, you can't go strictly on personnel either. This is a game of emotions and we took our shot in a funny way.

We got out to the Coast on Friday, and Saturday afternoon a bunch of us went down to the Bull and Bush to watch the Colts-Packers game. The Colts won big, and when it was over we were getting up to leave when someone said, "Wait a minute. Let's see what Shula has to say." Shula was still coaching the Colts then.

Frank Gifford came on to interview Shula and they started talking about the big Colts-Rams game for the following week and how it was going to be THE GAME of the year. No one even mentioned that the Rams had to play us first. They just passed over it as if the Rams had already won. It was a fore-gone conclusion. We didn't count in anyone's thinking. We were just a tune-up for the Rams.

This game was as important to us as it was to the Rams and I could see that all this talk about the Baltimore-Rams game was really getting everyone pissed. Finally O'B jumped up, snapped off the TV, and said, "Why those SOB's. We oughta go out and play them today."

We stayed steamed up and went out and beat the Rams. We held them to sixteen points and we got seventeen. That took care of all their talk about the game of the year with the Colts. Our beating the Rams gave the Colts the division title before they even took the field, and knocked the Rams out of the playoffs.

Ever since, whenever Dooley has said anything about holding a team to seventeen points I've been a believer. He said the same thing before our first game with the Vikings this year. We did our job. We held them to exactly seventeen points. And we beat them.

Besides, we know we can beat the Vikings. Their defense scores most of their points and if our offense doesn't give them any fumbles or interceptions and doesn't get pinned back deep in our territory we can beat them.

By the time we've gone over the Vikings' offense and the defenses we're going to be using against them, half the day is gone and it's time to break for lunch.

The guys spread out all over the locker room on chairs in the meeting room, even in the exercise room, opening their bags and bringing out their sandwiches. Everybody brings his own lunch, if he wants to eat. When we were at Wrigley Field there were a few hamburger stands close by and Martell and Freddie would take orders and run out and get sandwiches and shakes.

I pull some folding chairs together while Doug and Bru go to the lockers to get the lunches and we have kind of a defensive team picnic. This is one of the more glamorous aspects of the job, eating your lunch out of a brown paper bag close to your jockstrap.

Lunchtime is when I like to ask O'B about roasting the lamb. Ed's Serbian. His father put the O' in front of their name so he wouldn't be confused with all the other Bradoviches in Chicago. Actually I think Ed claims to be Macedonian since he heard of Alexander the Great.

A couple of times a year they spit a lamb and roast it and I like to discuss the proper procedures with him. Actually the big discussion is over garlic. Ed maintains you shouldn't use any garlic, and I always tell him you have to be lavish with it. "That's Italian," he always snarls.

After a hearty repast we hit the field. First come the calisthenics. Stanley's limping on a bad knee so he helps me watch the rest of the guys. We just do what we can without putting any strain on our knees. Everybody whacks the blocking sleds a couple of times and then we break down into special units.

The linebackers and deep backs run through the ball drill while the linemen keep hammering the blocking sleds. Shinnick

84

plays the role of quarterback, and one by one the linebackers and deep backs run backward, always with their eyes on the ball.

Shinnick pump fakes and every time he moves his arm you have to respond to the motion. Then he finally lets it go, over your head, to either side, low in front of you, and you're supposed to catch it.

All I can do is stand there and watch. It's frustrating and boring. I get the same kind of feeling I had in summer camp, not being a part of the team, being an outsider. We're getting ready for the last game of the season and I still can't run, and every time I try to do something that damn Astroturf makes my knee ache like hell.

It's time to break down into the pass and run drills. Dooley takes the first team offense and runs our pass offense against our first team linebackers and deep backs who are lined up in the Vikings' defenses. They're mostly zone now too. They don't use that bump and run as much as they used to.

Abe is down at the other end of the field with the second team offense running the Vikings' running plays against our first defensive line.

Then we switch. We go down to Abe and the second offense runs the Vikings' pass patterns at us and the first offense runs their own running plays against our first defensive line and some backup and taxi squad guys filling in as linebackers and deep backs.

Dooley keeps hollering that he wants a picture. "Give us a picture now defense. C'mon, give us a good picture."

Abe patiently snarls at the front four, telling them the little things they ought to be watching for that will tip off the play.

Everything goes by the clock. Fifteen minutes for this, and twenty minutes for something else. Dooley keeps the time and blows the whistle. Most teams work about fifty-fifty on offense and defense, but because we've been having so much trouble scoring we spend most of the time working on the offense.

We try and make everything as authentic as possible. Abe and Shinnick tell us what mannerisms and tips to look for; how a guy might line up a little different or vary his stance depending on where a play is supposed to go. They even have the quarterback use the same kind of count the Vikings will be using, a rhythmic or a nonrhythmic count. In a rhythmic count the quarterback calls the signals in a steady beat; hut–hut–hut. In a nonrhythmic count the quarterback calls the signals without a predictable tempo: hut–hut–hut-hut.

Abe does most of the talking. He keeps on the guys to be ready for the quick count and then hold it, not to get too anxious and go offside on a longer count. He says we've got to be ready to go the minute the center puts his hands on the ball. Shinnick is quieter. He talks more to the individual instead of the unit.

Dooley blows his whistle and the whole team comes together for the eleven-on-eleven drills. The offensive runs their stuff at a full defensive team now instead of just backs and linebackers or just a line and linebackers. Then the defense takes over. We run our regular defenses, some special line stunts, and our red dogs.

Against the Vikings Sunday we'll be changing our line and our formations quite a bit. I'll be calling a lot of audibles and dogs, and we'll be using both the zone and the man-to-man. It feels good to be out there running the stuff, even when running means walking.

We're pretty well organized and we get through our stuff really fast. We try to hang on to whatever we can, keep together, although things have gone from bad to ridiculous now. We've just about lost everything there is that makes a team, and it's hard not to go along. We can all see we're not going anywhere. It's the offense more than the defense. Abe and Shinnick have done a good job keeping us together.

But the offense, they fool around at practice and somehow they find an awful lot to laugh about. I can't but they clown around and they haven't scored but one touchdown in the last four games. I'd hate to be seen laughing around the locker room or on the field if I was an offensive player. Dooley and the rest of the offensive coaches certainly aren't handling it.

I argue with myself about whether I should say something, but if the coaches can't or won't do anything about it I'm surer than hell not going to be able to. That's the kind of guys we've got. If a guy's not going to think of the team before himself, well . . . All there is is the team. The individual is nothing. That's what the game is supposed to be all about. But those guys treat it as a big joke. To lose is one thing, but to be utterly disgraced week after week, that's something else. I want to be able to hold my head up win or lose. But how can I?

It's not just one or two individuals. It's a kind of creeping futility that sets in. But if we can't score touchdowns we're not going to win. And to those of us who are on the field the whole damn game playing defense while these guys come in and run three plays and punt, well I can't see what's so damn funny, not when we can hardly walk during the week. No wonder they win dance contests.

It's a long day, our longest of the week, and maybe I just get sick and tired of standing around most of the day shifting from foot to foot. By the time I take a shower and walk out of the locker room it's after three thirty and I still have another fight coming up with that traffic on the Dan Ryan Expressway.

After supper I started to give Nikki and Ricky their baths. I filled the tub, threw them in, handed them some soap and wash cloths and told them to get busy. They're both old enough by now. I went down and set up my projector. When I got back about twenty minutes later they were still in the tub playing around. Those kids really like water. I had to practically tow them out of the tub. I wrapped them in towels and shagged them into their own rooms to get dressed for bed.

Then it was Matt's turn. I brought him in and he had a pantsful. I took care of that chore with all his wiggling and squirming and then put him in the tub. Some soap got in his eyes and he started screaming. Helen just stayed in the kitchen making cookies. I finally got him quieted down and turned him over to his mother.

That's it. Now I was in the proper frame of mind to watch Tinglehoff and those guys knock Lucci on his ass.

6

Thursday, December 16

The only good thing about the day is that it's defensive day. It's relatively short to begin with, and Dooley shortened it up even more this week. Before I went out I had Freddie Caito give my knee a real good rubdown then I heated it up in the whirlpool and had him bend it good and hard to see if we couldn't force a little more flexion into it.

Ed came in and sat down. He just came back from the doctors. He had some treatment on his ribs, but even though it's his day he still doesn't know if he's going to play Sunday. It'd be a shame if he couldn't. But what the hell, if it wasn't his day he'd have no reason to play.

Out on that damn Astroturf my leg started to bother me again. We got through our stuff real fast. We get our stop defenses; second and seven plus, third and six plus, long yardage situations where the coach takes out a rush man and brings in a fourth linebacker, or takes out a linebacker and brings in a fifth deep back. As soon as we were finished they let us go and we didn't have to hang around while the offense stumbled around.

I jumped in my car and headed for Rupcich's, a restaurant at 106th and Indianapolis Boulevard, close to the Indiana state line. The Skyway took me past and above good old Chicago Vocational High School, CVS. I could see the old triangle field where we used to practice when I was a freshman. That was fourteen years ago, half my lifetime. I had to laugh to myself.

Of all the old memories that could have come to me, the one that popped into my mind was the one about the three guys in the car.

I had just started going with Helen. She lived a couple of blocks away, and I was introduced by a buddy, Rick Richards. People who think I'm kind of quiet and withdrawn now should have known me in those days.

Helen was standing in front of her house with a girl friend and Richards started talking to the other girl. I just stood there, feeling self-conscious, shifting from foot to foot, looking at the sky, the clouds, the trees, the grass, and kicking clumps of dirt with my toe. It got so that every day Richards and I would see them outside and every day he'd talk and I'd shift and gaze.

I had a yellow Cushman motor scooter and I thought that was pretty big stuff. So one day I said to Richards as he was heading toward the girls, ask her if she wants a ride.

So Richard said, with a jerk of his thumb toward me, "Dick wants to know if you want to go for a ride?"

She looked at me kind of funny, and then smiled and said, "Okay, I guess so."

She got on and we rode around for a while and I brought her back without ever saying a word to her. Every day it was the same thing. Richards would ask her if she wanted to go for a ride, and we'd go through the same thing. One day on the way over I told him to ask her if she wanted to go to the show with me.

Everybody must have thought I was crazy, but I just hated to talk to people I didn't know. Don't ask me why. When she said yes, she'd go to the show with me I figured she really liked me. I think the first thing I ever said to her was, want some popcorn? She said yes, and I felt like the ice was broken. After that we started dating regularly, but for at least a year after that her mother swore that I couldn't talk, that I was born dumb.

Helen used to wait for me every day. She'd sit in my car parked along the curb next to the practice field and read a book or something while we went through our drills. For a couple of days I saw the same car with a couple of guys in it driving real slow and then take off whenever I came out. I asked Helen who

89

they were, but she said she didn't know them. I was kind of hot-tempered and possessive in those days and didn't like the idea of someone fooling around with my girl.

One day right after practice I saw them cruising real slow and stopping next to Helen. We were working on punts but I completely forgot everything. When I saw them I started running. I didn't know what I was going to do. I was in full uniform, the cleats, the pants, the hip pads, the shoulder pads. Even as my spikes were clattering across the sidewalk they still hadn't seen me, but the car started to move. I saw the front window was open, and I'll never know what made me do it, but I dove head first right through the open window.

It was a two-door car, and there were two guys in the front seat and one in back. My lunge carried the guy in front into the driver. I had him with my right arm, I was kicking at the guy in back, and I got my left arm around the driver's neck, grabbed the steering wheel, and wrenched it to the left.

We were all scrambling and struggling and went up over the curb and just missed a lamppost, and the driver slammed on the brakes just before we went up the front stairs of the school.

There were all kinds of kids in front of the school and in front of the store across the street. Everyone gathered around. Someone opened the door and we all came rolling out. The policeman on duty there broke it up, with help from the coaches.

They jumped back in the car and drove off. I walked across the street to where Helen was sitting, and a big crowd, including the team, followed me. Bernie O'Brien chewed me out a little and told me I could have been injured doing a crazy thing like that.

That's a crazy thing to remember, I suppose, but that's where it really all began, at CVS. That's when I really became aware that my whole life was being focused toward athletics.

Football had a special claim on me though. All my brothers played. John, the oldest, played at Fenger. Ron at Tilden and at Illinois, and with the old Chicago Cardinals and in Canada for a couple of years before a knee injury knocked him out. Don was a fullback at CVS, and Dave played there too. One of them was always in a game somewhere, and I'd always tag along and watch and listen to the older guys.

When I got to high school I felt like I was there to prove myself. We went to CVS mostly to play football. My brothers Don and Dave were there before me, and they and some of the other guys in the neighborhood told me that Bernie O'Brien was a good coach and that they were going to have some good teams.

We had a pretty good frosh-soph team losing only two games. I was a tackle on offense, and on defense they had me play over the center. The next year I made the varsity. I played strictly defense, the nose guard over the center, but I was allowed to roam a lot, much like a linebacker.

The next year I was switched to fullback. The way it happened was right out of the old Knute Rockne movie. We were fooling around in spring practice and they called a tackle-eligible play, a pass to me. I caught it and made a pretty good run. The other guys started kidding me about switching to fullback. That summer our regular fullback joined the Navy, so I asked Coach O'Brien if he'd let me try it and he said okay.

The fullback was the big man in O'Brien's system. He handled the ball on about seventy-five percent of the plays. I did some passing and all the kicking—punts, place kicks, and kickoffs. On defense the fullback played linebacker. That was my first real shot as a linebacker. I loved it.

I guess it was then that I realized how much I really liked the game and first got the idea that there was a definite future for me in football. But I didn't really know how far I could go. I was afraid to think too far ahead, afraid of setting myself up for a big disappointment.

I had no one to measure myself against. Aside from my brothers, I never followed anyone. I never really paid any attention to anyone else or had any heroes. Although Coach O'Brien would talk to me from time to time and tell me that if I worked hard I could make a fine future for myself.

I wish my kids could be raised the way I was. But they can't be. No way they can be that lucky. We were constantly being tested by both others and ourselves. We always had to force ourselves to measure up or be left behind. We were resourceful enough to always be able to entertain ourselves, and we only developed respect for the guy who could do things, instead of just talking about them.

Besides, they're going to have too much. We weren't poor, but we weren't rich either. My father had a good trade, he was an electrician, but with seven kids to raise there weren't a lot of extras.

There have been very few really rich kids who made it big in sports, especially football. They might make it in some other sports, like golf or tennis, or something like that, but football's too tough if you don't really want it. Maybe those kids have a different sort of competitive mechanism. They don't need material success. On the other hand I don't completely agree that sports is the sure way out of the ghetto either.

It's almost impossible to pick out a high school player and say he's going to make it as a pro. There are just too many things he has to overcome. Only about one high school player in seventy makes the team in college. Then narrow that down to one of the starting eleven or twenty-two. There are injuries and financial problems at home that can knock a kid out. He can have trouble with his class work or want to get married. Or maybe he's impatient to get the things that money, even a little money, can get him right now, like a car and clothes. So he sacrifices his future.

Money wasn't that important to me. When we were young we entertained ourselves. We'd go to watch Ronnie or Don or some of the other older guys play football. Our spare time was completely taken up by sports. No one had a car. And we worked. I doctored up my birth certificate when I was fourteen and went to work as a furniture mover and loaded tile at a tile company down the street. I even made a competition out of that. I'd drive myself to do as much as the grown men I was working with.

One thing I've noticed now in life, now that I've had time to think things over, is that the men and women who succeed are the ones who pursue their goal with a single-minded determination. Keep driving and never stop. Desire and determination. Like Abe says, desire and determination supersede every other attribute. If you've got those you'll win, no matter how long it takes.

92

That's why it's hard for me to understand guys who say they hate to practice but like to play. To me there is no difference. I always find myself asking the same question, are they so satisfied with themselves that they don't think they can improve?

I've never really, inside myself, been satisfied with anything I've ever done. I want to do well not only for myself but also for everyone watching. I have a deep sense of obligation to the fans. If nothing else, I at least want to put on a good show for them. That's why I've always said that I want my last game to be my best, because they always remember your last game. That's why deep down I really care about Sunday. It's my last game, for a while.

Maybe all this sounds naïve. I know when I went to college everyone thought I was naïve as hell. A lot of guys used to jag me about not getting any money. I could have had that. One guy, who claimed he was a recruiter for Indiana, said they'd get me a new Corvette, or any car I wanted. Some other guys took me to an expensive Michigan Avenue tailor and had them make me a suit and topcoat. I told them they had no chance, that I had already given my word to Illinois. Those are the kind of values I learned at home from my mother and father and in the neighborhood.

All Illinois did for me was get me a job in the summers and help us find an apartment when Helen and I got married. I still had to pay the rent. They also helped Helen get a job in a bank.

I didn't even know they gave anybody money. I learned better later. I know a couple of guys who got scholarships for their girl friends. Other guys had alumni sponsors and could always count on having a little extra cash.

If I got hurt and couldn't play, or didn't make the team, I didn't want to feel obligated to anyone. A lot of guys would brag about what they were getting. I didn't believe most of them. Hell, half of them weren't playing. If they were getting what they said they were, they were cheating someone. I just felt that I was fortunate to be going to college. I wasn't looking for money or anything else.

My greatest asset though was my luck. I raised a lot of hell, even after I knew I had a clear goal. A million things could have

93

happened to me. My first year I wanted to quit every day. Our line coach, Bill Taylor, saw me through it.

For the first month or so I had a roommate by the name of Bill Eisley. He was another hell-raiser. The worst thing that could of happened to either of us was to become the other's roommate. We used to take motor scooters and motorcycles out of the student parking area and go for rides. The police were always chasing us.

One night we were riding around on a motorcycle and the campus police tried to stop us. We were roaring over the lawn near the library and I was trying to stay close to the trees so the squad car couldn't follow us, when suddenly this low-hanging branch was almost in my face. I ducked but there was no time to yell. Eisley never knew what hit him. He was knocked cold and clean off the bike. I kept going. I finally ditched the cops and hid the bike. When I got back Eisley was just starting to come around. The cops drove right by him in the dark. I laughed and he moaned all the way back to the dorm.

My best ploy was the "pizza trick." I'd call a pizza joint and place an order for the fraternity house across the street. I'd give him a made-up name and a room number. When the truck would pull up and the driver got out to make his delivery we'd go into the truck and help ourselves.

One time it backfired. A bunch of us were sitting around the room and I announced that I was getting hungry. Bertetto knew what I had in mind. Taliaferro started to count his money, but I told him he wouldn't need any. Like a big deal I strutted to the phone and made the call. The truck came. The driver got out, and we helped ourselves.

We had a good time laughing and eating, and when we finished Taliaferro said it was only fair that since I treated him to dinner that he did the dishes. He gathered up all the scraps and headed for the garbage can.

He opened the door and then slammed it. He opened the closet and started throwing all the dirty cardboard plates full of tomato sauce all over my clothes.

"Hey, what the hell you doing?"

94

"The delivery guy is right out in the hall," he whispered, making faces to be quiet and jerking his thumb over his shoulder.

Everyone started scrambling for the waste baskets. The guy saw Mike, but when he walked in I was acting innocent, sitting at my desk pretending to be studying.

"You guys are pretty stupid," was the first thing he said.

"Huh, what are you talking about? Who are you?"

"In the first place you should have pulled the shades. I could see you from the sidewalk. In the second place, before you try and act so innocent you ought to wipe the sauce off your chin. C'mon, pay up."

I started laughing and he started laughing. But supposing he called the cops instead of coming in himself. I could have been on my way back to Chicago. And people would say, for a few years anyway, "Oh, yeah, I remember him. What's he doing now?"

"I don't know. He's a furniture mover I guess."

But Taylor nursed me through. He gave me tips on how to study. He encouraged me to work hard in class, and he predicted just about everything that eventually happened. He said the first year would be a rebuilding year, but that before I graduated we'd go to the Rose Bowl. He said I'd make All-American and sign a big pro contract. He was right on every count.

It's funny, the things that can run through your mind in quick flashes when you're driving alone. To see the old school like that. But it looked so dirty and dingy. I guess it's the dirt from the mills. It's a great big school and it used to be a nice, light yellow brick. All the windows are broken in the machine shop now.

I thought of all the times we used to go out and have a few beers after a game. We'd drive all over the southside and just goof off. Going over the 103rd Street bridge I remembered how Helen and I used to go to the 103rd Street beach on hot summer nights. We'd drive over in my Plymouth coupe. I cut a hole in the roof and had the hood shaved and painted it a nice metallic green. It had whitewalls and those big hub discs we called moons. I bought it for something like a hundred dollars with money I made working on construction jobs.

95

It looked good until somebody stole my hubcaps when I was at practice one day. We spent a lot of time at that beach. Just looking out at that dark water and talking about the future. I was talking to Helen by then.

The lamb was roasting at Rupcich's, and some of the guys were already there having a few drinks. There are only seventeen guys on the defensive team plus the two coaches, Gibron and Shinnick. Buffone didn't come because he had a virus, and O'B didn't come because his back was bothering him. When I got there, just to keep the peace, I called Helen and told her I'd be home right after we ate.

We were standing around the bar waiting for the lamb, which Abe decided he better supervise, being a Lebanese and all that. Smitty, our strong safety Ron Smith, who calls himself the Gingerbread Man—you can run and run as fast as you can/you can't catch me I'm the Gingerbread Man—I've heard him saying it to himself when he's getting ready to take a kickoff or a punt—Smitty and I started telling some of the rookies stories about the good old days.

The first team party I ever went to was just before we broke camp in August. The excuse they used was that it was Bob Wetoska's birthday party. Wetoska was an offensive tackle from Notre Dame, one of our captains, and a helluva nice guy. I didn't think there was anyone on the team who didn't like him.

A pizza and beer party was a longstanding team custom. And being the kind of guy I am I just looked at O'Bradovich kind of sideways when he was saying in the locker room, referring to me, "I don't know if we ought to invite the kid over or not, the rookie." And they'd talk about whether or not I was fit company and things like that just to jag me, and finally Ed said, "All right, come over to the pizza joint in town. We're going to have a party."

I said, "Okay," but didn't pay much attention to him. I really didn't know what was going on because I was a rookie, and a loner besides. I didn't think it was any big deal. I don't think he even told me it was Wetoska's birthday party. So after practice I just thought, the hell with it, and went over to the cafeteria. As soon as I got there, though, I knew there must be something wrong because I was the only one in the place.

I went through the line and all the serving women were asking me where everyone was. They're at a party, I guess. While I was eating all by myself in that big, empty hall I got lonesome and I figured, what the hell, I might as well go on over.

The party was in full swing. I was the only one who wasn't there. There was a table heaped with all kinds of food and a big tub full of iced beer. Everyone seemed to be having a good time. I went to the back of the room and talked a little bit to O'B, Marconi, and Richie Petitbon. Frank Budka was holding down center stage.

Budka played quarterback at Notre Dame and he was trying to make it as a defensive back. He was challenging all comers to a beer chugging contest—just open the can and see who can drink it down the fastest without spilling any.

I sat there watching and he beat a few guys, and then someone started hollering, hey, get that millionaire in there. Get that rookie in there. And O'B and Richie said to me, "What do you think? Think you can beat him?"

"I don't know. He looks kind of fast, but I think I can beat him."

So they start hollering, "Here's our guy. He'll beat your guy." And they were pushing me up to the front of the room. Somebody stuck a can of beer in my hand and another guy said, "Ready, on three! One! Two! Three!"

I beat Budka hands down, or bottoms up, and then Richie and Ed, my two promoters started screaming, "All right, all the rookies have to take a crack at Butkus for the championship."

The next guy was Brian Piccolo. I don't know when he started drinking, but it must have been like the day before. I could have chugged a gallon while he was drinking an eight-ounce glass. He was that slow.

Then I went through everybody, one after another, all the rookies, and then my promoters, Richie and O'B, were hollering for the veterans to step up and take a crack. Me doing the work. Them making the money. These two guys were sitting in the back nice and dry and sober running a book and cleaning up on me.

97

Everybody was getting blind. They were really getting blitzed. Some guys were walking around demanding a rematch and Richie and Ed were telling them to wait their turn. Business was really good for them.

Everyone was getting smashed but I was staying level because of my meal in the cafeteria. All the rest of the guys were drinking on empty stomachs after a day's practice in the hot sun. Your body wants fluids. So drink down a couple of fast beers and then *bamm.*

Half the guys were staggering around trying to get some food into themselves until someone said, "Hey, it's seven thirty. We have to get back for the meeting."

Big Doug Atkins lumbered up to the front door and just filled it with his body. "No one leaves," he roared. "No one's going to any damn meetings." And he meant it. Now Doug is about six-foot eight, and about two hundred seventy, and no one was inclined to argue with him about it or try to force their way past him because he isn't only big, he's incredibly strong, one of the best-built big men I've ever seen.

Everybody started hollering at him, "C'mon Doug, we gotta go to the meeting. We'll all get fined. We'll come right back."

Finally he let us go, but only on the promise that we all come back and finish the party after the meeting.

We had quite a parade going back to the meeting. Guys sitting on the hoods and roofs, and the horns blowing. I drove my car, a brand new Riviera, right up the steps of the dorm.

We staggered into the meeting rooms upstairs, the offense in one and defense in another. Budka had one of those long, blue plastic stadium horns and he was blowing into it, making that horrible noise, and we started to sing—

> Hooray for Halas, hooray at last,
> Hooray for Halas, he's a horse's ass.

The door flew open and there stood the Old Man. Close to seventy years old, and he was in a rage. Budka never saw him, half the guys didn't. They were still on the third chorus.

The Old Man, bad hips and all, roared across the room,

ripped the horn out of Budka's mouth and started beating him over the head with it. Budka was trying to hide, to cover up, to get away, and every time the Old Man hit him on the head he'd sink lower and lower in his chair, until finally he was on the floor.

In an absolute fury the Old Man started wading up and down the aisle swinging that horn left and right, belting everybody who couldn't get out of the way, and shouting, "You're all drunk you no good dirty bastards. You're all fined, you rotten sons of bitches."

I don't know what made him stop, but he finally did and stalked out of the room. We all sat there, stunned. George Allen came in with his neat little list of corrections and got the meeting over in a couple of minutes. Then it was back to the pizza joint.

This time Atkins brought a jug of what he called Fighting Cock. It tasted like that big hillbilly made it himself. He made all the rookies drink a half glass and that really speeded things up. Evey was getting goofy because he can't drink anyway.

Everybody started beating their chest and arguing back and forth. The defensive guys were telling the offensive guys how horseshit they were and the offensive guys were saying how horseshit the defense was. We almost had an unscheduled intra-squad game right in the pizza joint. We probably would have torn down the joint if someone, it was probably the owner, hadn't warned us about missing the eleven thirty curfew.

O'B and Richie decided to continue the party in O'B's room so they brought back some pizzas and six-packs. We were all in the room drinking and eating and laughing. We thought we were being real quiet, but when you've been drinking you only think you're being quiet.

The door was almost knocked off the hinges, and for the second time that night the Old Man was in a rage. But this time it was a cold rage. Just looking at his face I could see then why everybody said he was a tough old bird.

He stood there coldly looking around at everybody in the room; and nobody said a word, and then he said, "All right, you no good bastards. You're all fined."

He hadn't seen me yet, because when he opened the door it

screened me from him. But when he turnd to go out and close the door he saw me sitting on the corner of the bed, up against the wall. And when he saw me he completely changed.

"All right, all right, young man," he said. "You shouldn't be associating with bums like this. They'll just get you in trouble. You better go to your room now." He closed the door and left.

"Holy Christ," all the guys started saying. "If it wasn't for big boy here we would have been fined for sure." Then they started calling me coach's pet and saying Halas was my sugar daddy.

That all came back as we were standing around waiting for Abe's lamb. These guys thought the stories Smitty and I were telling them were really hilarious. I was thinking how much more glamorous everything sounds when it's a couple of years old and wondering what kinds of stories these guys would be telling rookies a couple of years from now.

This was a tame party, though. We had a few drinks and had some lamb. Nobody got rowdy or made any speeches. After we ate we just cut out. I brought Bru along back to my home. Sam Miller, a good friend of mine who's Matt's godfather, was over and we shot a couple of games of pool and then I told Helen I had to drive Bru home.

But I couldn't take him home without first stopping at Stuka's and Flea's, a couple of real, honest neighborhood workingman's taverns. I had been telling him about these places for a couple of years now and promised I'd take him in if he ever came south to Roseland.

Stuka's is a joint where if Stuka doesn't happen to like you, the way you're dressed, or the way you look, he'll tell you to get the hell out. Shots and beers, no mixed drinks. If you order a fancy drink he'll tell you to go someplace else. If you play the jukebox and he doesn't want to listen he'll pull the plug and tell you the place is for drinking, not a dance hall. Flea's is the same way. A phony wouldn't last a minute.

We ran into Rick Richards and Ed Shill, another old buddy of mine in Stuka's, and we drank some beer and bullshitted with them and played some bumper pool, and before we knew it it was closing time.

7

Friday, December 17

They were driving down the field. It was a third-down pass play to someone else. Walking back toward our huddle I looked back to see where everyone was, to see if anyone was wide open. He was walking back toward us, all of a sudden he started to stagger and fell to his knees, then his hands, then he just sprawled out. His face was toward me. Everyone thought the guy was faking, stalling for a time-out, but I saw his eyes . . . they were rolling back. He couldn't fake that. I turned and signaled the Lions' bench. The officials were coming over, then they were running, the doctors were running. They were working on him, trying to get his heart going, pounding on his chest with their fists.

When they carried Chuck Hughes off the field I knew he was dead. I thought, if I had to go, that's the way I'd want to go, right on the field because, there is nothing else I want to do. That guy died right. But I started thinking that this can happen to anyone, at any time. I sad a prayer for Chuck Hughes. Our Father who art in heaven . . . I never thought of the words like that before . . . I said a prayer for all of us. Hail Mary full of grace . . . It was like the first time I ever spoke those words.

I thought of Brian Piccolo's last game. We were in Atlanta . . . just blew another game. Some guy, a lineman, even ran back an on-side kick for a touchdown against us. It was hot. My locker was right near the Coke machine. I was getting out of my uniform. Pic came over. He was starting to have trouble. He had a

*bad cough, he had chest pains. He was swigging a Coke. I said,
"Hey Pic, let me have a drink." "No, you don't want a drink," he
said. "You might catch what I've got." He was half joking. Little
did we know that he had cancer. It came jolting back to me . . .
Said a prayer for Piccolo . . .*

*Thought of other things too. What if I had hit Hughes on a
pass route? Or what if I was one of a group of guys who hit
him? Gang tackled him? What if I was involved in any way?
They took my picture. I was standing ten or twelve yards away.
But it looked like I was standing right over him, hands on hips.*

We won the game. It was a real big win for us, but Hughes'
death was such a tragic thing that it took all the excitement out
of the victory. The following day Ed McCaskey, our vice-presi-
dent, Cadile, Willie Holman, Dick Gordon, Bob Wallace, who
had been a teammate of Hughes at Texas El Paso, and myself
acted as the Bears' representatives at a requiem mass in Detroit
before they took his body home to Texas for burial.

Joe Schmidt, the Lions' coach, came over and thanked us, and
so did the owner, Bill Ford, and the general manager, Russ
Thomas. What hypocrites.

When I got home that afternoon I found a magazine that
someone sent me. There was a story on the Lions' middle linebacker, Mike Lucci, quoting Ford as saying, "Something ought to
be done about that Butkus. He intentionally tries to hurt people,
and that's wrong."

Schmidt was also quoted saying that I definitely try to hurt
people, whereas when he was playing he never tried to hurt
anyone. Russ Thomas was quoted as saying that he's talked to
the Bears about me. He said he told McCaskey I ought to be
barred from football because I definitely and deliberately try to
hurt people.

And then the center, Ed Flanagan, says that I use abusive
language and I'm a dirty player. Lucci said, "We used to be
friends. But now Dick won't even shake hands with me before
the coin toss at the start of the game, and I'm just as good as he
is, and I'm not saying he's bad. He's a good one, but I think I'm
as good with Detroit as he is with the Bears. I thought we were

friends. We always had a few beers together whenever we met..."

That really got me. That Schmidt and Thomas and Ford and Flanagan and Lucci. They're nothing but a bunch of lying cry-babies. That goddamn Lucci. He came up to me at the Brian Piccolo golf tournament last summer and he was trying to pump information out of me on how to negotiate a contract.

"What do you think I should ask for?"

He's quizzing me, trying to find out what I'm making. Then his front office tells him I'm making a certain amount and they want him to sign for the same thing. So he's trying to find out from me if they're lying to him. And you know they are. The dummy.

I'm damn sick of this whole Detroit situation. For the last couple of years now this Lucci has been trying to make some sort of reputation for himself by knocking me. I wish to hell he would try to make the Pro Bowl on the field instead of with his mouth.

No one but those jerks has ever called me a dirty player. I play as hard as I can. I try to hit as hard as I can. To me that's what the game is all about. But no one before has ever called me dirty. They started this thing, Joe Schmidt popping off about Lucci, how great he is.

Truthfully, I don't see how they can rate Lucci that high. There are at least a half-dozen guys around who are better than he is: Mike Curtis of the Colts, Nick Buoniconti of the Dolphins, Tommy Nobis of the Falcons, Willie Lanier of the Chiefs, Lee Roy Jordan of the Cowboys, Al Atkinson of the Jets, and Lonnie Warwick of the Vikings.

It annoys me when someone says that anyone is as good or better than me. Call it ego if you want, but it just isn't true. No way. I watch some of these other guys in the movies and man, they get downright embarrassed. I've seen Lucci get run right off the field. It irritates me because I know it's not true. There are so many idiots who believe Howard Cosell and believe any-thing they read. And then if we lose all the time it just reinforces their beliefs. They say, well this guy must not be doing his job.

That's why no matter what the score is I play just as hard as

103

I can. There is still your own pride. There still might be one smart guy in the stands saying, well, they might have been bombed, but that guy is still playing. There is still one guy still standing with his head up at the end.

Not like Lucci. They're winning, but when the other team scores you see his ass getting blown out of there. That's what I try not to let happen. Try not to get beaten badly on any play no matter what the score. Because if you start dogging it and someone else looks at that movie they can still say something, even if you've had a great game up to that point. Then they can say, if he was doing his job they wouldn't be scoring so much. That's why it was such a great thrill for me the first time I was named Defensive Player of the Year, to be singled out like that even though the team had a one and thirteen record.

This whole thing with Detroit started a couple of years ago. We were playing in one of the first Monday night telecasts. Mel Farr was running the ball and we had him stopped, but he was still standing, so I figured, what the hell, and tried to take the ball away from him.

They had an isolated camera on the play and from that angle it looked like I was hitting him with a karate chop. But I wasn't. I was going for the ball. That's where it all began. But hell, the referee was standing right there. If I was really doing anything he would have dropped the flag. You know how many penalties I've had called on me this year? One fifteen-yarder.

When I got home after the mass I started going through my mail. I knew it would come, the hate stuff. The first one addressed, Dick Butkus, Murderer. It was scribbled in pencil. Curiosity made me open it. Some quack was saying, Well, you finally did it. You finally killed somebody. Aren't you proud now? You're going to get yours sooner or later. Of course, there was no named signed, but it was postmarked Detroit.

I wasn't going to read anymore, but another from Detroit was typed and had a return address so I opened it. It started by the writer saying he lived in the Detroit area and was a Detroit fan and a Lucci fan.

He said he never thought much of the Bears or much of me. "But my opinion of you has changed after the tragedy involving Chuck Hughes. After seeing you wave and trying to get the doctors out there I've completely changed my feelings and ideas about you and the Bears." At least he left me with the idea that everyone in Detroit isn't a jerk.

I was the first one in the locker room. I sat in the whirlpool for about ten minutes until Freddie Caito came in and then when he got ready I laid down on the table and had him rub the leg again.

"Freddie, just jump on the goddamn thing and bend it all the way. That'll either fix it up or I can get out of here a couple of days early." He gave it a pretty good snap and then I hit the weight machine again.

It was cold and snowy and icy and the Astroturf was slippery when we went out, but the leg felt really good. And I was thinking to myself that this has to be one of the few games I've ever gone into that by this time of the week I wasn't able to feel it building inside me. Maybe it's just because it's the last game of the year and we're not really playing for anything.

It's different now with me than it was when I was a rookie and for my first three or four years. It's not so much that my attitude has changed, it's just that I can control my emotions so much better now. During my first few years I used to take the pre-game warm-ups just as seriously as the games.

I never smiled, goofed off, or even talked to anyone. I used to look at the other team just to try and catch some guy smiling or laughing and I'd use that to get myself worked up. I'd use anything I could to get myself worked up—newspaper stories, the boo's, something, anything some guy on the other team might have said, even if it was years ago.

You play the game on your emotions. You have to have them working for you. For me I think that my emotions have more to do with any success I've had than any physical talent. I can turn my emotions on and off in competitive situations and use them to help me. When I'm playing I can get myself excited over almost nothing and reach a peak quickly. It doesn't take much for me to get teed off. Sometimes I make some of it up—if a guy looks at me the wrong way. It could be any kind of reason. It could be something I saw someone do when I'm watching the films.

105

I invent feuds to get myself up. It doesn't matter who it is. It doesn't even have to be anyone in particular. It can be a mannerism someone has. If I hear someone said something, or I read something that refers back to me I use that to get myself up.

Thinking back to previous games helps too. Whenever we play the Colts I like to think back to one game where they scored over fifty points on us and still tried to kick a field goal in the last minute.

Sometimes when I tackle a guy and want to agitate him a little more I get up by pushing down on him. I always say something to them when I'm climbing off. The first thing that pops into my mind. Any little thing. I try to make a big deal of it for myself and hope it carries over to the rest of my teammates. At times I go into the defensive huddle still calling some guy an SOB trying to stir up our guys.

When we played the Saints a couple of years ago they were the first ones on the field for the pre-game warm-up. A lot of us were as sick as dogs. The night before we ate in some of those fancy New Orleans gourmet restaurants. Buffone, Cadile, John Johnson, myself, and a bunch of other guys spent the night with our heads in the sink.

We came out mopping and dropping. Then I heard a couple of the Saints yelling back and forth to each other, "Oh look, here come the big bad Bears. Oh, how big and ferocious they are." I turned to see who they were. I couldn't tell, but I wanted to thank them. That's all I needed.

I walked over to some of our guys and said, "Listen to those jerks calling out all that crap." I kept harping on it trying to get them worked up.

I remember everything. I remember Dan Reeves. After the game when the Packers beat the Cowboys in that icebox game they asked Reeves about Nitschke. He said, "I don't know why they're comparing Nitschke with Butkus and Tommy Nobis. I've just played against the best. They can't compare with this guy."

That burned me. Reeves never played against me so how could he really know or make comparisons. But people took his word that Nitschke was the best. So I remembered that and used it to get myself ready for our game with Dallas the next year.

I had a pretty good day. I managed to give him a couple of pretty good shots, and every time I hit him I'd talk to him. Just called him a couple of names, told him what a lousy runner he was, and I'd say, "Jeez, I wish I could be as good as Nitschke." Just good clean fun and kidding around.

I yell at the referees too. But only if it's a close call and I think we have a legitimate gripe coming. That keeps me going too. I can keep doing it, but after a while, after we've played about twelve games or so it's more of an effort. We play all those exhibition games and I try and play them the same as a league game. So by the end of a season I've been wound pretty tight.

I scream at the refs, but I don't believe in taking my troubles to them, or going to them for protection. I can defend myself. But some guys are always bitching to the officials.

One game with the Rams, the game we beat them and knocked them out of the playoffs, O'Bradovich was bitching all day long that their tackle, Charlie Cowan, was holding him on every play. I told him to take it out on Cowan instead of going to the officials.

Maybe it payed off though. They finally caught up with Cowan and dropped the flag on him in the closing seconds. It came on a completion that would have set them up in field-goal range with only about fifty seconds to play and trailing 17–16. Instead they had like second and twenty-eight from their own forty-seven.

I got a big kick out of reading the Los Angeles papers the next day. They were screaming at the officials for misplacing a down, giving the Rams second and twenty-eight instead of first and twenty-eight, and about the penalty to Cowan.

They were bellowing that the refs are supposed to overlook such minor infractions as holding and call only flagrant violations—like murder, I suppose. They claimed that this was the first time in his life, practically, that Cowan ever committed such a misdemeanor.

What a joke. After the game O'B's arm seemed to be six inches longer than the other.

Now, after being in the league for a while, instead of turning myself on during the pre-game warm-ups I can go along and enjoy myself right up to the kickoff. It's not only the year we're having, but it's also that I know so many more guys around the league. My first couple of years I didn't know anyone. I didn't talk to anyone. If anyone talked to me I'd give him a dirty look and ignore him. Now I even talk to opposing players and coaches before the game.

The first couple of years in the league you concentrate on your own assignment and don't allow yourself to let your attention wander from it. You try and overcome your mistakes by aggressiveness. Maybe you play a little more out of hate and rage. But as you go from year to year you find yourself developing a coolness. Now and then I even find myself smiling and cracking jokes in the huddle.

I can read a lot of quarterbacks now just by watching how they place their feet when they're behind the center. Some line up a little bit differently depending on what they're going to be doing. If a quarterback's feet are even, he's going to go one way. If his left foot is back, he's going to go that way. If the right foot is back, he's going to drop back. Some of them even drop back differently depending on which way they're going to throw the ball. It just takes experience and a quarterback who doesn't study his own moves on the game films.

I try and look into the huddle to watch the quarterback's mouth and read what he's saying. That way I can catch the play number and the count. Most teams have similar numbering systems for their plays so that way I know what the play is and I can put our team in a defense that will make the quarterback call an audible, or I can let him go ahead and run the play if I feel pretty sure we can stop it.

Joe Kapp, when he was with the Vikings, was one guy I could read all day long. I'd stand there on our side of the line of scrimmage and look into their huddle and plain as day I'd hear him call the plays. I bet I caught 80 percent of their plays this way.

One game I looked into the huddle and heard Kapp saying, "Draw on two, draw on two." They got up to the line and I started hollering to my guys, "It's a draw, it's a draw, watch the draw." I even called an odd-man line to get a man over the center to make it almost impossible for them to have any success with that play. They ran it anyway and Bill Brown broke it for about twenty yards.

Milt Plum was another guy I could read easily. One game I got at least the count on every single play. I was standing in the hole every play and was able to get a good jump on the red dogs.

So most of the time it helps, but one thing I've learned is that when I get a tip it's best to keep it to myself. If I know where a play is going I can call an audible instead of hollering to my teammates. That way they won't be looking around and thinking about what's coming. They'll be concentrating on their own assignments.

I enjoy that part of the game as much as any, the finesse and strategy that is as much a part of the game as the bodily contact. If it was just matching strength, the strongest man would win every time. It's also being smart enough to maneuver players and teams into situations where you can use your strength against their weakness. That's as much a part of football as blocking and tackling.

That's why I always laugh to myself when some mother tells me, oh, my son is bigger than you are. Boy he should really be good. I don't care how big he is, he's got to have the desire. They've got to know what to do with their size, and not many do. And they've got to want it, really want it, and even fewer do that.

On the field we reviewed everything really fast. We put in a special goal line defense. I'm going to get into a three-point stance over the center, Mick Tinglehoff, because in watching the movies Abe noticed that the Vikings like to run a quarterback sneak when they get down close to the goal line. I'm supposed to submarine under Tinglehoff to jam up the play. Then we just run through our regular situation defenses, our third-down defenses and our red dogs. And that does it.

And after the unsigned letters came saying you finally did it, you finally killed somebody, it started me thinking, the generation where they just loved to see guys hit people, where they got their rocks off watching contact had given way. Now its don't say nasty words like kill, or kill 'em. What if that special they had on me, all those shots making the game look as violent as possible, had come out this year? Imagine all the things they would have said about me. Got hate mail then. What would it have been after Hughes?

It seems they were just waiting for someone to fit the role. I came along and they hung that animal tag on me. Everything, television shows, newspapers constantly build up this idea of how hard I play; that story about how I dream about knocking guys' heads off, knocking them right off . . . and all that crap. What if I would have hit Hughes? It makes me shudder, turn cold. Those reporters would have loved it—you finally killed a guy . . .

In college coaches and scouts used to call players animal. This kid is an animal, or that guy is an animal, or so and so is a beast. Beast was very big in their vocabulary for a while. Neither of them were meant to be derogatory. They were terms that were used to describe someone as a helluva player, a special kind of player.

It doesn't bother me now, but it did in college. I didn't like it, but I couldn't think of anything I could do to stop it. At best, I'm only mildly communicative. I just wasn't able to express a lot of my feelings. Besides, who'd want to listen?

I probably knew, or thought I knew, that it was a somewhat complimentary way of referring to my ability on the field. But in my case it more or less carried over off the field too. I was able to live with it most of the time, but when that story in *Sports Illustrated* came out, that really screwed me up. Then it really took hold. The writer, Dan Jenkins built it up as much as he possibly could, way out of all proportion. He made me look like a stupid, lumbering ox.

It's my own fault because I trusted him. I should have known better. I was afraid it might happen. I knew how things could be twisted out of shape, how they can make you look ridiculous. I asked the photographer, I asked him if this guy was all right. Otherwise I wasn't going to say very much. And he said, "Yeah, he's good. He'll only write what you say, the way you say it."

When Jenkins asked me why I went to Illinois I gave him

the most honest answer I could—to play football. I had a chance to go to a lot of schools, most of the big schools and even a couple of Ivy League schools but even if I had gone to Harvard my answer would have been the same.

I told him that even though I didn't particularly like classroom work I did it because it was necessary if I was going to accomplish my goal. I said a lot of people set goals for becoming doctors or lawyers but very few of them fulfill those goals.

Something happens along the way and they peter out, or else they really didn't want it bad enough to begin with. I said that was why I felt I was doing a good job in getting what I really wanted in life. I wanted to play professional football and this was the road to it. That was why I was in school doing the work. Not that I liked it, but because I had to do it to accomplish my goal. For the first time in my life I talked too much.

He twisted it to make it come out that if I wanted to be a doctor I would have, but I was too dumb, so I became a football player. What I said was that if I wanted to be a doctor I would have worked at it just as hard as I did football, but I didn't want to be a doctor, I wanted to play pro football.

That really got a reaction. He made it sound as if Illinois was just pushing football players out the back door. Pete Elliott and I had to go see the dean. He said that story was a disgrace. He said it was an insult to the university. He made it sound like I was Jenkins' partner.

From then on they made it as tough as they possibly could for me in class. All the instructors took the story as a personal attack on them. They decided to show me the real benefits of an education.

It was then that I decided to have as little as possible to do with reporters and magazine writers. I started to really resent being called an animal. I resented it my first couple of years as a pro. I didn't like being described as someone who walks on all fours. Worse than that, to me at least, it implied stupidity. I didn't like the idea of not being able to read without moving my lips, or having to sign my name with an X.

On the field you practically have to act like an animal. You're propelled by your baser instincts, or at least what are thought of as your baser instincts—hate and rage and the desire to inflict pain and punishment. Some show it more than others, but just about everyone in the game has it to some extent. A defensive back or a running back or a split end may have the same emotional charge but they seldom get tagged with that animal business. They just don't seem to fit the idea as much as a linebacker or a lineman.

No matter how long you're in the league you can still develop that hate once the whistle blows. And each guy has his own way of mustering it up. It's not a personal hatred. It's more an anger or madness you have for anyone you come in contact with. It's not directed at any one particular guy, you hate them all equally, unless it's a Lucci or some other loudmouth, a Flanagan, or someone like that.

I want that competitive hatred burning inside my guts. I hope that I don't get as lenient as some guys do after they've been around a long time. They get so blasé about everything it starts affecting their play. That's what I can't understand. When you're all stirred up inside, when you're on, you fly to the ball and hit with all your might. If a guy's stumbling or only halfway down you still want him all the way down to finish him off.

That's what competition is all about. It's the killer instinct. You have to have it. You have to have it if you're playing golf, tennis, polo, horseshoes, ping pong, cricket, and even chess. When you have someone in trouble you have to put him away. If you don't you just give him a shot of confidence and he'll come back and knock your head off. Anybody who has ever competed in any sport, or in life, will tell you that. When you have them on the hook hang them. Joe Frazier is praised for having a killer instinct, but when I say I have it I'll be criticized.

You want to hurt, but not injure. There's a distinction, in my mind at least, between the two. I want to flatten and intimidate my opponents. I want to absolutely destroy them. But I still want them ready to go the next day.

I don't think I'm the most popular guy on the field. That's all right. I'm not trying to be. I don't want them to love me. No one ever sees me smile, or pat an opponent on the back and say, nice play. Why should I. He's the enemy. For those sixty minutes I hate him. If he made a good play so what. He's supposed to make them. He's a pro. That's what he gets paid for.

Why should I encourage him to make more. It'll only hurt me and my team. When a guy puts a block on me I want to kill him, not congratulate him.

Listen, all those guys who are always helping the runner or the quarterback to his feet are a bunch of phonies. They aren't doing it out of any sense of sportsmanship or anything like that. They're just trying to rub their noses in it a little bit more. It's like saying to them, here little man, I knocked you down and now I pick you up. I can handle you just as I please. It's just a different form of intimidation.

Flanagan's always crying that I swear at him, the poor little fellow. Well, when someone's holding me I don't just say, hey, please don't hold me now. I say the first thing that pops out of my mouth, and it's usually some reference to his birth or training.

Swearing is just another release out there. Everybody is swearing at everyone else. It isn't choir practice you know. When a guy's holding you and trying all kinds of crap in a game and the ref isn't calling him on it you've got to do something. You can't hit him in the head even though you'd like to, because then the ref will drop the damn flag on you.

Then on Tuesday when you see the game films and you aren't making the plays you're supposed to, what are you going to say, are you going to cop a plea and say, look, that guy is always holding me? Well, it doesn't do any good on Tuesday. You should have done something about it on Sunday.

Maybe that guy is watching the film at the same time you are, only instead of copping a plea he's telling everybody, look at that dumb bastard. I held him the whole game and he didn't say a damn word. Then the next time we'd play he'd try to get away with even more.

You've always got to protect yourself. In Denver they'd throw a block and then slip off and try to tackle you or grab your ankle, or trip you. As long as the refs don't call it guys are going to try and get away with anything they can, anything you'll let them get away with.

Bitch, bitch, bitch, I'm always bitching. Got to try to keep more of these things to myself and not always be bitching to Doug and Ed and Bru. But I can't help it. All kinds of things get

113

under my skin. It just comes out. People think nothing ever satisfies me. Well, hell, I didn't make the world. When I see something going on that I know is wrong, what am I supposed to do, keep my mouth shut? Or say they're right, just so people don't think I'm bitching all the time.

But on the other hand there's a lot to be said for bitching. What if Ralph Nader hadn't started bitching about the automobile industry? What if people hadn't started complaining about the pollution of the air and water and the despoiling of our natural resources?

What changes would have been made in the war, the political system, the way the schools are run if the young people hadn't started screaming?

That's what brings progress about. If everyone kept still even though they could see all sorts of wrongs there'd never be any changes. Good, constructive bitching means progress. That makes me a progressive, not a bitcher.

Every jerk in the world must be driving today, and somehow they all manage to get in front of me. Guys doing about thirty miles just stay in the left lane and won't move over. They were irritating the hell out of me. I felt like driving right over the top of them. And looking at the dirty street and depressing gray sky didn't help either. It makes me wonder what the hell I'm doing here. Is money really worth it? Living in this kind of atmosphere, dirty and slummy?

Can't wait. Just hope there is nothing wrong with the camper. Everything is geared for Monday. How would I feel if we were winning? If we were in the playoffs like we thought we'd be in the mid-season? Florida would be a long way off then. I've got one more game. Give it a real good go. Really fly at them and end on a good note. Then down to Florida.

Helen has to come with me to get the camper because she has to drive the car back home. It gave us a good chance to make our final plans. I told her she ought to think about bringing her mother down with her. She could help take care of the kids and make it a little more of a vacation for Helen. We talked about taking the kids out of Montessori school here and enrolling them down there. That would give the kids something to do every day. Besides, they'd meet other kids, new kids, and that would be good for them too.

There are a lot of things we can do, so why stay up here in the cold when we can be enjoying the warm Florida sun. The only thing holding us back is the kids' school.

I told Helen she'd need her mother because after I relax for a week or so I've got to be on the move again. I have to be in Miami to make some training films the first part of January, then I might have to go to the Pro Bowl the middle of the month, and I have to be back in Chicago the end of the month.

So I told her, "Heck, you can have your mother come down and help with Matt. That way you'll have some time to hit the pool with Nikki and Ricky. Somebody has to keep an eye on them and you can't watch Matt and them too. Besides, it'll be a little vacation for your mother too."

That'll be good for both of us. This last week the kids have really been getting on her nerves. With the cold weather they're in the house all the time. When they go into one of their bratty moods they definitely don't listen. When they're in that mood they don't even listen to me. I wonder who they take after? So maybe the best thing to do is go down to Florida and let them outside and work off some of that energy. Let them waste it outside instead of running Helen down and running me down and getting us into arguments.

It wasn't such a bad ride after all. The dealer was a very friendly guy. He went over the whole camper with me and told me what he did to it, what problems he had. He said I might have a little trouble with it in the wind.

I've got the camper. I'm self-contained. I'll have everything I need in there. I'll stock in a little beer and a little wine, so what more could a fellow want? This way I can drive down and have plenty of time to think. I can do eighteen or nineteen hundred miles of thinking and see what's going on along the way instead of trying to race down there.

Tomorrow I'm going to have to start getting order in the house. Get everything packed and lined up. Got to go to a meeting tomorrow. Drive all that way again just for a lousy ten minutes to go over the same stuff we've been going over for the past six months. Our game plan is so simple I don't even have to go over it. I know it. But what the hell, an animal has got to have something to growl about.

8

Saturday, December 18

One more. That's all, one more. One more practice. One more day. One more game. One more season. Gone.

Not one season. Two seasons. Two different seasons. Not being able to practice or get in shape, and then to have a game like that against Pittsburgh. Winning it like we did in the last couple of minutes.

We thought my leg would get force bent in the game. It wasn't. I still didn't have any flexion when we went to Minnesota. Of course nobody picked us to win, they're one of the powerhouses. They had us down by eleven points in the fourth quarter and with their defense. But Kent Nix came in, he threw one score. We need five to win. Get the ball, get the ball, c'mon defense, get the ball.

Down by four, we kicked off. Just a couple of minutes left. We pinned them deep. We stopped them. Everybody was up. Everybody was keyed sky-high. We did the job. We stopped them three straight plays. They had to give it up. We had position. It felt great to do the job like that. It felt like we were a team. With only seconds left, on fourth down, Nix threw for another touchdown. It felt great to be a winner.

Osborn was going off tackle. We hit him. Gang tackled him. He was rolling. My leg was beneath him, it started to bend. I felt it stretch. I yelled. Doug grabbed him, pulled him off. Osborn hollered, "What the hell." "You okay?" Doug asked. "Yeah, yeah, it didn't really loosen it any."

We got to L.A. and called Jimmy Caan. He played Piccolo in the movie *Brian's Song*. Called him, and Doug and O'B and I went over to his place in the afternoon. Took us on a tour of Hollywood and Beverly Hills. Got Don Rickles on the phone, we insulted each other for awhile. Jimmy took us to lunch. Met him for dinner.

It was warm. It was hot in L.A. It must have been ninety on the field. That was good for my leg, the heat loosened it real good. We were on grass, that gave me better movement. The defense played well. I got a couple more interceptions and a fumble, but Concannon got hurt. It was his knee. Operation, out for the year. Nix couldn't do it this time, not three in a row. They fooled us with reverses, end arounds. But on one of their scores Holman was definitely clipped. It was right out in the open. They didn't call it, the movies showed it plain as hell. But you win or lose on the field on Sundays, not in the movies on Tuesdays.

The knee just seemed to reach a plateau. It wasn't improving, but it wasn't going downhill. It was just kind of maintaining itself. It still lacked flexion.

I can't hurdle people. Can't do something and then react over a mistake. Make a mistake and it's twice as long in recovering. It's frustrating, nothing I can do about it. Just got a late start, as it was I was lucky.

We had New Orleans. They were playing real well. Our offense had a good day, we contained Archie Manning pretty well, just concentrated on keeping him inside. Don't let him get to the outside. O'B hit him a real good shot. He had to leave the game. We won pretty easily. Went out to Frisco three and one.

Everybody was high, talking it up. We had a wild kind of enthusiasm, which we haven't had since we won about nine in a row my rookie year. You can't explain it. Practice is fun. It's over too fast. Everybody wants to stay out on the field to do a little more. Everybody's hustling. Everybody's friends. Everybody's pulling for everyone else. You don't think of yourself, you think of the team. What you can do for the team. Guys find excuses to come early, hang around the locker room after practice. Everybody walks with his head up. Winning is fun, you can take pride in it. You know you're doing your best, that's what life is all about. You try to be the best at something, not as an individual, as a team. You know that if you win it's because you made a contribution.

If you make a big play you feel that much better. The team needs you, depends on you. It's another challenge you have to meet now. You look at yourself on the films, there's always things you do wrong, always things you can do better. No one says anything about it when you win. But you know, you know inside yourself. You want to do better. You don't just want to do your job, it goes deeper than that. You can always get better, always improve, but it's something you can't conquer. You can never be perfect, but you have to try. You have to strive for it, and when you win it makes your striving that much easier.

We played well again in Frisco, held them to thirteen points. A touchdown and a couple of field goals. We got an interception on Brodie and about four or five turnovers. Concannon was out already, then Nix broke his thumb. The offense couldn't get going. We missed a couple of field goal tries and never got a point on the board.

In two games we lost two quarterbacks. The Lions were waiting for us in Detroit. They thought they could win the division. Dooley moved in with Bobby Douglass to prepare him for the game. Everybody laughed, called them the odd couple. Everyone wondered where Bobby hid the broads. Larry Walton ran back the opening kickoff for them about a hundred and two yards, but that's about all they got. Our running game went real well. We all played well, then Chuck Hughes died. They didn't seem to want to play after that, we didn't either, but our momentum carried us through.

Dallas, the Cowboys were next. They have so much material it scares you. They made lots of yardage, but inside the thirty or twenty we tightened up. They just couldn't score. We got a couple of fumbles. Dikta dropped an important third-down pass. They missed a couple of field goals. Percival hit on his. It seemed like every time they got the ball they were deep in their own territory. It just seemed they drove and drove and drove. They gained four hundred and some yards on us, but every time they started a drive it was eighty yards to score.

They scored right off the bat, then we tightened up. They

were shuffling their quarterbacks every few plays, Morton and Staubach. Douglass had a real good game. He scrambled for one, got it real close for another. We got some turnovers, it was just the way it's supposed to be played. We complimented each other, got them in good field position.

Their offense has all that motion and all those formations, for once we simplified it. We just rotated to the wide side of the field no matter what they did, that way we didn't get confused trying to make a move every time they made one. It worked.

A couple of years ago we got bombed by Kansas City 66–24. Dooley had the bright idea of matching every move they made. They used the I formation and lots of motion and all kinds of different sets. We got so confused with our own moves they ran all over us. For awhile we simplified things, but then we started getting complicated again. We were saying, Jeez, if we ever play Dallas it'll be all over. But we simplified it, worked on it all week. We knew what we were doing, ignored all the different sets they threw at us.

We got some breaks, Dikta dropping that pass. We got a couple of interceptions. Thomas left the game. Hill was hurt. Garrison did a good job, he's a good back. Our offense was able to score. We gave them good field position. It seemed like the whole game was field position. Each time they had to start deep in their own territory. They made the mistakes.

The calls for tickets after the Dallas game. I felt like changing my number again. An unlisted number didn't do any good. They got it anyway. Everybody was calling for tickets, not just regular season tickets, playoff tickets, superbowl tickets. All of a sudden we're the biggest thing on Earth. We're five and two, half the season's over, the toughest half. Everybody's talking playoff now. Everybody's figuring which games we ought to win for sure, how many we can lose. Dooley's telling us nine wins will make it. You beat Minnesota, Detroit, and Dallas and you can do anything. Let's see now, we'll beat Green Bay twice, Denver, that's all anybody talked about . . .

Wonder how those guys took it. Here we were just half finished. Wonder how a team like Green Bay took it for all those years. The pressure they must have had, the people calling, the tickets. Here. Go here. Go there. Speak here. Speak there. Make an appearance, we'd sure like to have you. You're our favorite. Maybe being in a small town helped.

We had it all. We were winners. We had the magic. We knew we could do it. We knew we could go along and go along and then all of a sudden explode and pull the game out. Green Bay was going to be nothing for us, except they beat us. We couldn't stop that trap with Brockington. I had a lousy game, one of the worst I've ever had. They said they neutralized me. Neutralized hell. I just had a lousy day. Trying to hand fight everyone, that's not me. Put your head and shoulder in there and go. We still could have pulled it out. As lousy as we played we still could have pulled out at least a tie. After I hit Hampton and recovered the fumble we tied the score, then we let the guy break the kickoff for about seventy-five yards. They kicked a field goal. Maybe if we stopped them deep we would have had time for another score. We had a cinch tie, but we let them break the kickoff. That's stupid.

Washington. Allen thought he was coach of the year. Dooley thought he was. They were going to run it at us and have Kilmer throw short and to the tight end. We were down all day, then late in the game we came on. We won it on a busted play. Douglass threw it to me, a thirty-yard pass for the extra point. We were back on top. We could forget about the Green Bay game. All week we all felt like hell for blowing that game. Now we were six and three, beating the Redskins squared us with ourselves.

Maybe it just caught up to us. Maybe everything just evened out. Maybe we had no business winning any of those games. Something happened, I don't know what it was. We played the Lions at home and gave them the damn ball game. We just weren't the same team anymore, the offense couldn't move at all. We let Landry break an option play for about fifty-five yards right off the bat. It looked so easy it was ridiculous. In the movies, they didn't show us anything different from the first game when we beat them. Gordon didn't play, which shouldn't have made that much difference. Staley was out with a bad ankle. Grabowski was limping. Hell, you expect to have guys banged up, that's part of the game. We couldn't move the damn ball. And, that goddamn Lucci, he intercepted three passes. He had one all year, probably had two in ten years. And that damn Douglass three, three of them right into his hands, right into his belly.

All week we were looking at each other and starting to ask, what's wrong? What the hell's going on? Don't find fault. Don't start placing blame. Just stay together, like Abe says, keep it together. Don't let it come apart, you'll blow the season. For too many years we've been two teams, an offensive team, a defensive team. One wants the other to fall on its ass, then they can point fingers. Don't let it happen now, we've come too far. We're still six and four. We've still got a chance. We've got Miami coming up, they're hot. If we can beat them we can still get up enough momentum to finish ten and four, that'll make the playoffs.

I had one of my bad feelings about that game. As soon as I got off the bus there were a bunch of kids and people waiting for autographs, then CBS wanted an interview, and then there were about five reporters. I don't like that crap before a game. I told them I didn't have time, then our PR guy, Dan Desmond, got hold of me and said just this one guy, so I talked to him.

Then that night we went out to the Orange Bowl for practice. The kids were yelling my name as soon as I got off the bus. They cheered and yelled my name and hollered all kinds of goofy things. It's embarrassing. What am I supposed to do? Wave and bow? Or what? Some guys it might make feel real good, but not me. I just don't like it.

They call my name and nobody else's. The kids come running up and people surround me. The fans bitch at me. Some guys say that all the reporters are afraid of me. Every year someone wants to do an exclusive. Some guy comes out and writes about the steel mills and interviews McCaskey. For a story on me, they hardly talked to me. Another guy stands on the sidelines and hears all the noise and just can't get over it. Every time a couple of pads come together he thinks bones are breaking. Or the guy who writes about grown men playing a boy's game. What does that make him. Spending all his time writing about a boy's game?

People don't realize how things happen. I got all kinds of mail on that *Playboy* story, the vulgarity, my image. Young boys reading it. Why are young boys reading *Playboy*? And then some people were surprised or shocked by the vulgarity. Some thought it was very truthful.

I come out of the locker and it's a mob scene, people singling me out and throwing things. It's just like building a monster. Now I'm going to have to face it, to live with it. I'm going to have to face the guys jagging me in the stands or picking me out in the plane or anywhere else I'm recognized. I didn't want that to happen. On the field it's one thing, but I don't like it to carry over to my other life. I try to avoid it.

And it was hot. And we ran under the first punt. And jeez it was hot. And I couldn't catch my breath. Coming from about thirty degrees to damn near ninety. But I was kind of glad, my knee would loosen up and all the aches would go away. And after practice Frank Gifford came over. "Hi Dick, Frank Gifford." "Yeah, I know." So he asked how I felt and all that and I just answered. I didn't volunteer anything.

The night of the game we got off the bus and all that hollering crap again. And Desmond came over and said Howard Cosell wants to talk to me. He said they want to do it right now, before the game. And I wasn't even taped, but I said all right. I might as well do it now and get it over with. They were going to tape it for later, when they were on the air. So I thought if he was going to say something I was just going to jag him back. I figured if I didn't he was just going to say some crap anyway. I had no idea what he was going to talk about an hour before the game, so I put on my pants and jersey and went out. There were people in the stands already, yelling and blowing those plastic horns. Yelling at me and yelling at Cosell. And he led off with about ten adjectives. Then he got into the big confrontation, between me and Csonka. One on one, that's the way it's been building all year.

I said I didn't look at it that way. They were both great running backs, Csonka and Kiick, and they had a great team. And we both had ten other men on the field with us. A bunch of kids were on the field for a punt, pass, and kick contest. And Howard started yelling, "Come on, get those goddamn kids off the field. This man's got a game to play." The cameras came in for just a head shot and he started all over again.

"You're looking at the epitome of linebackers." And he really pulled out all the stops, in that drawn-out nasal voice of his. And I was cracking up, because in the locker room Doug and Bru were giving it to me, imitating Howard Cosell.

"How good is Dick Butkus?" But-kus, the way he says it. And they pretended they were announcing the game. "There's a ten-yard short up. And oops, they're working on But-kus, working on his knee. He can't cover the short outs, Dandy. And they're getting to Jerry Moore, the young rookie from Arkansas. They're working on him, Dandy. The fact of the matter is Dandy that they're working on But-kus on the traps and draws."

So when he started that stuff, "And tell me truly Dick," I thought of the way Doug and Bru were imitating him with that drawl and started to laugh. But he was all right, except for pushing that one-on-one crap.

Running off the field back to the locker room the people started to boo and they were holding up signs. Hey Howard, who's Butkus? When we came out for the pre-game warm-up they started booing all over again. But it wasn't as bad as when I was being interviewed. And I just didn't feel right, doing that interview. It was like counting your chickens before they're hatched. I had no real reason to think that way, that's just the way I think at times—that these things will happen like that, that I'll put the hex on myself if I say anything before a game. That it'll come back to haunt me. I wasn't looking at the game as just stopping Csonka. They have more than one good runner. They have a helluva team. So when the game started the fans started throwing stuff at us, and it made me stop and think. They were throwing things right at our bench and nobody made a move to stop them, and it made me think. What the hell am I doing in front of these kind of people? Then I though it'll just give me more incentive not to get caught looking bad in the game.

It was real hot and we were on the field. Bang, bang, bang. Three plays and in we go again. We weren't getting any help from our offense, and they started scoring on us, and they were good. And every defense I called was the wrong one. Even if I did call the right defense they just threw into it one way or the other, or else Griese'd scramble and make a big play. But it was just a matter of getting beaten by a good team. That night they were a super team.

After the game there were more boos and people were throwing more crap, and bitching at me. And I was just thinking, man, what the hell is this? It's better to number ninety-nine at the end of the bench than put up with this crap. Doug and those guys. They never get it. They never catch that crap. It's just me getting it.

In the locker room I was thinking. Boy, those reporters are really going to lay me away, because it was supposed to be the big match-up, me and Csonka. Cosell said so. So I got undressed and a couple of them started over, but I just went in the shower and stayed there for a while. And I shaved and showered and it was so hot I couldn't stop sweating. I couldn't hide forever. As I was getting dressed they gathered around. Guys with pencils and guys with microphones. And I just said, "Hey listen, we just got beat by a great team. Csonka and Klick are great runners. Griese's a helluva passer. We just got beat tonight. There's no more. What more can I say?" And one guy said, "Did they do anything you didn't expect?" "Yeah, I didn't expect them to score thirty-four points on us. But they did." Then I just walked away.

It's always like that, if you win no matter what you did everyone overlooks any mistakes you might have made. But when you lose, when you get beaten bad, that bad, a lot of things go through your mind. You keep asking yourself, what the hell were we doing wrong? We weren't doing anything really different, or we're not executing right. Are a lot of the guys too tired? Can't they make themselves go a little more? Then you think, what the hell's wrong with the offense? Why are they throwing the ball? Why can't we establish a running game? How can a team like this . . . Here they've been in the league six, seven years, they've got a powerhouse. We're in it over fifty years and can't even make a first down on them.

Then I started thinking. Griese, the scouting reports on him were that he was too small, too fragile, he would never make it. Csonka was too big, too fat, too slow. Kiick, nobody ever heard of Kiick. Warfield they got in a trade, they stole him for a number-one draft pick. Our first-round draft choices end up on the taxi squad.

Everything goes through my mind. Fleming turns out to be their style of tight end, big, strong, and a helluva blocker. Lombardi said he couldn't block, he's sure doing it now, very seldom gets a pass. But when they throw to him he gets them. Demarco had an argument in St. Louis and Shula steals him. Little has to be one of the best if not the best.

All that stuff goes through my mind. Guys who come here don't believe our organization. They don't try to make a guy happy, that's what Steve Wright was saying. He said, "Listen, I might not be back here next year. If they don't make me happy I'll go someplace else because I know I can make it." I said, "That's a pretty good position you're in, me I can't do that. I'm locked up. I can say I'd like to go someplace else, but then somebody's going to say, you can't, you're Chicago."

What the hell good is it? All this goes through my mind, not on the field, not in the game, but when I'm walking off. When I'm sitting on the bench, all that goes through my mind.

And I just sit and watch Dooley calling the offensive plays. And when you talk to some of the offensive guys you find out they didn't even have a game plan. They used to send in the plays by note because guys used to forget the plays on the way into the huddle. They'd hand Douglass the note and he'd read it. For a while Howard Mudd was one of the messengers. He was going to send in a note. Palm one and once the game was lost hand it to Douglass. A loaf of bread, a quart of milk, a dozen eggs. We all had a lot of laughs talking about it, but it's really sad.

Going back on the bus we were sitting in the back. Shinnick came back there to talk about what happened, nobody felt like talking. We knew it was all over. He came back and said we should have done this or that.

A lot of the guys were just beat and tired and hot and Doug said, "Hey, the hell with this game." He's ready to quit. You wait all week to play the game and then you have to live with this until the next game. It starts to wear off in a day or two.

The shock wears off, but you have to relive it in the Tuesday movies. You never really know how you played until you see those films. You wait kind of like in limbo until you see the movies. You never really know until then, no matter how you try to evaluate yourself it's just a blur.

Denver, what would you call it? Debacle, that's the word. Three games without a touchdown. Neither team scored a touchdown. We missed all kinds of easy field goals. It must have been one of the worst games ever played.

Everything is wrong now. It's so ridiculous, so frustrating, so goddamn frustrating. When we saw the films we all said, "Man that Denver's bad." They were playing without Rich Jackson and some other regulars. We beat them easily in the preseason. Maybe we all thought it was going to be easy, and then we couldn't even score one touchdown. We lose six to three. Everybody blitzes hell out of us.

Dooley had a great idea. Bring some of those bull horns down to the sidelines, that way they could warn our quarterback when the blitz was coming. Can you imagine that, standing there on the sidelines with a bull horn to warn the quarterback when the blitz was coming. He had Martell pack four of them, but he didn't use them.

After that disgusting disgrace nobody gave a damn anymore. The rumors started that Dooley was on his way out, supposedly he had to win to save his job. For the first time this year they started bitching on the sidelines. Bitching because they wanted him to take Douglass out and put in Nix. He stayed with Douglass all the way. He got dumped on his ass nine or ten times. I just stopped watching in the third quarter.

How the hell did it happen? How the hell did we beat Minnesota, Detroit, Dallas, and Washington? We were five and two when we beat Dallas and six and three when we beat Washington, and now we're six and seven and we can't score a touchdown. We can't even kick a twenty-yard field goal.

We play Green Bay again and the passer with one of the worst records in the league, except for ours, of course, has a field day. We fall down to give them easy touchdowns. Bart Starr wears gloves and still completes passes, and nobody gives a damn. That's what kills you inside, nobody seems to give a damn. Well I'm here now anyway. At least for a while I can keep my mind occupied. Soldier field, home of the Bears.

Everything changes in a few weeks, a few months. When we came here after Camp Burnham Harbor was full of boats, everything was sunny. It's the same as our season. We thought we were really going to do something. This was going to be our year, and now all the boats have sailed. After Sunday our lockers will be as empty as that yacht basin.

9

Sunday, December 19

What's the date? The nineteenth. Just a couple of more days till winter. That's funny, our first game with the Steelers was on the nineteenth too. Darker now though. Almost no sun. Depressing weather. Don't think about it. You can live today, you can play today. That Tinglehoff better look out, I feel good today . . . I feel fast today . . .

The kids are up already and having a ball. As soon as they started school they started getting up early every day, and now they won't stay in bed. All right, listen you kids, Nikki, Ricky, get those cookies out of the parlor. If you want to eat go in the kitchen.

Check to see if Helen put the steaks out, put some money in my envelope, holler in to Helen that the kids are up, and then head for the car.

Getting near church now. Father Murphy is a pretty nice guy. He came to Ma and Pa's fiftieth wedding anniversary, drank some beer with us. It's a big church, but not many people come out. It's a poor parish.

It's pretty empty. So few people attend mass here that they have half the church roped off. I sit in the back along one of the ropes. I like to watch the people come in and see how they act. A girl and guy come in, both about seventeen or eighteen, and dressed like hippies. No one else pays any attention to them. I guess if they really were hippies they wouldn't be coming to church.

All through the mass I watch the people. I like to watch their actions and try and guess what's going through their minds. I always notice the way people kneel. Some of them get lazy, and instead of kneeling they half sit and half kneel by slouching back into the seat. Men seem to do it more than women. I wonder why.

The sermon goes right over me. I sit there thinking about what kind of week it's been. I'm afraid I haven't been too easy to live with. Thinking back I could see that all I did was bitch and moan. Everybody does it, even winners. I must be the worst in the world though. I've got to cut that stuff out though because it puts you in the wrong frame of mind. Everything looks sour to you.

The last day . . . the last game. Give it everything you've got. Make it something to remember.

I leave right after communion. My last prayer is not that we win, it's that no one gets hurt, Bears or Vikings. I play as hard as I can, but never to injure anyone.

These guys think they're going to the Super Bowl. I doubt it. They don't have enough offense. They live off their front four, those four guys Page, Eller, Larson, and Marshall make that team. The rest are good, but those guys make that team. Get in front and they have trouble. I doubt if they'll get to the Super Bowl. But hell, what am I talking about? At least they win. When was I with a winner last? . . .

Helen has the eggs and toast on when I pull into the driveway. After seven years her timing is down pretty good. Nikki and Ricky are still running around. I take over the two strip steaks while she corrals the kids and gets the table ready.

A blocker is coming at me. I drop him with a forearm. Huumph. I just kill that Tinglehoff. Pow. Knocked him right on.

130

Sweep! Sweep! . . . Ummph. Spin 'em . . . get 'em get 'em . . .
Ummmph. Look in his eyes. He knows . . . He's scared. Dog dog
. . . Ummph. They won't touch me today. They won't . . . I
won't be blocked today. When they hit me . . . like running into
a brick wall.

Turn the steaks over to sear the other side. Helen has the
eggs, juice, and toast on the table and we all sit down. Matt
bangs on his highchair. Nikki tells me that steak is her favorite
food. It makes me feel good, not because Nikki likes it so much,
but because I can proudly ask myself, how many kids get steak
in the morning?

When I was a kid, even on Sundays after church, we had
soft-boiled eggs. We'd crack the shells and scoop the eggs into
a dish and tear off pieces of toast and mix it with the eggs. I
still have that for breakfast Monday through Saturday, but Sundays are different. Sundays are steak days. Sundays are game
days.

After breakfast I take the paper and head for the bed for a
short nap. Just riffle through to see what some of these guys are
saying about us, see if I can use any of it, and breeze through
Kup's column to see what's going on around town. I get through
that stuff pretty fast and then it's time to lay back, close my
eyes, relax, and think about my old pal Mick Tinglehoff.

If that SOB comes out and holds me I'll give him a rap right
away. I'll give him a forearm right in the head. That'll let him
know what it's all about, or if he does hold me . . . maybe the
next play I'll almost forget the ball and really give him a rap.
Then I can go and try to make the play. No, better not go out
of my way. Make sure I get to the play. Plenty of time to get in
a shot or two. I can see him now behind his mask. Funny, some-
times I can recognize guys easier on the field behind their masks,
or the way they get in their stance, or the way they walk or run—
their mannerisms—than when I meet them off the field.

Hell, I could recognize that Tinglehoff anywhere, even in the
dark. Recognize his grab, his hold . . . like fingerprints, no two
alike. That damn guy holds me a lot. At least he tried to last
time we played. Wonder if he holds everybody? Of course a

*couple of centers claim I accuse everyone of holding. If I'm
blocked it's because somebody held me. That's the way I feel.
I should never be blocked. Nobody has any business blocking
me. If they do, well they have to be doing something wrong.
Holding me . . . clipping me . . . doing something illegal.*

Thirty minutes, even when you're dreaming about Mick
Tinglehoff, doesn't last long. Now it's up and get dressed, say
good-bye to Helen and the kids and take the long ride. I had to
get the bottle of champagne.

At the defensive party we decided that if Jerry Moore even
comes close to an interception, if he even touches a ball, we'd
crack open a bottle of champagne to celebrate. He's the free
safety and he's somehow managed to go through the entire
season without making a single interception. He's had some
balls right in his hands, but one way or another he's been able
to drop them all.

I told Helen about the tickets for O'B's dinner and told her to
take them and meet Vern Buhl in the parking lot after the game
and go to the dinner with them. I wanted to be able to take my
time and didn't want her hanging around outside the locker
room.

The kids are waiting to see me off. They say, "Get the ball
and win the game," because Helen taught them to, but it's a
funny thing, I can never get Nikki or Ricky to say anything else
to me about football. Sometimes I catch them talking about it
with other kids, but whenever I'm around they just won't talk
about it. Once in a while I try to coax a little something out of
them, but they're too smart for that and they just avoid it. Helen
says that when the games are on TV and I'm gone they'll sit and
watch. It makes me wonder what goes on in those little minds
and what I was thinking about when I was their age.

It's the last game, the ending of the year, a year I never
thought I'd have. I started thinking about how miserable it was
trying to play with my leg messed up the way it was. I always
thought that I'd never see the day when I'd admit to myself
that I didn't like playing, or that I was tired of it, or that I was
glad a game was going to be over, or a season was going to be

132

over. But this time I was because I wasn't able to play the way
I wanted.

*This feels like the last ride. How many years now? Seven.
This is the end of the seventh year. Next year will be eight.
When I started I told myself, if you can just play five years that
would really be something. Then I said ten . . . I wanted to play
ten years. I used to tell guys I'd play ten years at middle linebacker and then switch to center. What I really want to do is
play till I'm sixty and then take my pension. Why not? If you
work in the mills you work till you're sixty or older and then
take your pension. Why not in football? It's all I ever want to do.*

*But I want to win too. In the seven years I've been here we've
come close once. The best record we ever had was in my rookie
year, 1965. We won about nine in a row. Sayers had a fantastic
year . . . about twenty touchdowns . . . six in one game against
Frisco. Rudy Bukich led the league in passing. The only trouble
was we lost our first three. We were out of it before we got
started.*

*The next year, 1966, we thought we were really going to go.
I pulled a groin, Johnny Morris, our best receiver, got a knee
early in the year, Andy Livingston never made it back from his
knee, Atkins was gone in the expansion pool. We just couldn't
get it going.*

*In 1967 Dooley was the defensive coach. Kansas City scored
over sixty points. That Indian rides the white horse around after
every score . . . that horse was so lathered up we thought the
Indian would slide off. When we had a little offense we didn't
have any defense. Opening day we had Pittsburgh down thirteen
zip and we got bombed out. It ·was Joe Fortunato Day in Pittsburgh. In Cleveland we held them to a field goal most of the
game. Knocked Frank Ryan out. One time the offense had third
and sixty-two. Unbelievable . . . we beat the Cardinals and
Giants bad. The Giants were pitiful. Frank Cornish, all three
hundred pounds of him, even intercepted two passes on Fran
Tarkenton . . .*

*The next year was crazy. Sayers got hurt, Concannon got hurt,
Virgil Carter got hurt. It was the first year of the new divisions.*

133

We would have won if we beat the Packers the last game. You know we blew it.

Nineteen sixty-nine was either a joke or a bad dream. We were one and thirteen. Everybody beat us, even the Giants. That's how bad we were. Unbelievable fluke plays. Concannon takes his hands from underneath the center. He calls a time-out. It was supposed to be a quick count. Pyle snaps the ball. It sails over Concannon's head. A linebacker catches it in midair and runs about seventy yards.

A tackle runs an on-side kick back for a touchdown. We block a field goal try. The kicker catches it and runs for a first down. Crazy fluke plays. Carter calls everybody chickenshit. He ends up at Cincinnati. What a year . . .

Then last year. Erratic. Sayers hurt again. No offense. Defense on and off. Had the Colts down seventeen to nothing and blew it. Didn't get the zone down, but finished strong . . . gave us hopes.

Soldier Field, it's early, but the cars are already coming in and the people are walking to the stadium carrying lunches and Thermos and something extra. It must be pretty tiring sitting in those stands all those hours in the cold so I hope I can do something to stir them up.

Sometimes I get the idea that they're Romans on the way to the Coliseum, coming to watch the gladiators and the big cats do their stuff. Sometimes I wonder just what role I play in their imaginations.

The kids are there waiting. I suppose they're the same everywhere on earth. They start hollering and I hear them yelling, "There's Butkus." Some just say hello, and the real meek ones won't say anything. They swarm around. They want an autograph, or they just want to touch you.

I don't see what the big deal is all about. During the game there's some reason for it, but not before. It just makes me feel funny. I don't see any sense to it. Kids aren't so bad. I like kids, but it's the adults who do it who get me. Because they can get at you away from the stadium too.

I really wonder what everyone does with all those autographs.

Every time I'm out some place and people come over and ask for an autograph, I always wonder how many of them would really take the trouble to write if they really wanted one.

You go into a place and someone recognizes you and comes over and asks for an autograph. Then he sits down and you see someone he's with lean over and ask, "who's that guy?" So he tells him, and then the second guy comes over and starts talking to you as if he's known you for years. That's why it's getting to be a pain in the ass.

I come out of the locker room after a game and they're going nuts. After some of our early games I thought they were going crazy. The Pittsburgh game, the Dallas game, the Washington game, it was a madhouse out here.

Then some lady sends me a letter after the Pittsburgh game. She said I didn't sign her son's autograph book and he waited all that time after the game for me. So I sent her a letter saying, gee, I'm sorry. I didn't mean to make you feel so bad. You know it was right after the game and I have to apologize. I should know better than to be thinking about the game right after the game. So here's a picture for your son. It's just too bad you couldn't send a letter asking for one instead of complaining that I passed him over in a mob.

I've found that people who really appreciate them write to the Bears' office and I'm happy to send them autographed pictures. It really offends my sense of dignity to see all those people jumping around like they're crazy, acting like a pack of jerks. You end up signing your name on match books, bar napkins, scraps of paper.

The real bold kids stand right in front of you when you're walking, trying to stop you. That's an old trick handed down by one generation of kids to the next. Almost every year the faces change, but the tricks are the same. But if you stop you'll never get in the locker room. I keep moving, walking fast. They get out of the way. I haven't stepped on a kid yet. I sign some autographs as I go. I never ignore them because I'm thinking about the game. I haven't even got my game face on yet.

"Dick, can you get us into the game?" some of them ask. I put my arm around a couple and tell the cop at the gate they're with me. Once they're in the gate they're on their own. Of all the kids I've gotten in that way I never did find out what happens to them once I'm in the locker room.

The rookies have been in the locker room getting taped for at least an hour before the veterans arrive. I go straight to my locker. Doug is there, and most of the other guys. A lot of them are talking about what flights they're going to be taking home.

I find Martell and tell him to send me some equipment and my uniform down to Miami because I have to do a training film down there after the first of the year. It's a new kind of film, film loops, and I asked him to pack the stuff in a box and mail it to me down there.

I gave him a check and he said thanks, and I folded the other checks and slipped them to Bernie Lareau and Freddie Caito while they were busy taping guys. I meant to give them all some money from time to time during the season instead of waiting until the end, but it always slipped my mind.

Some guys don't give them anything. They get paid by the club, but not for all the little things they do for you over the season. It's not a tip. I feel they have it coming.

As soon as I got undressed I walked over to the trainer's room and lined up to get taped. There's a lot of fooling around and playful shoving with guys hollering and Bernie shouting that if we don't shut up he's not going to tape any of us.

When my turn comes I jump up on the table. First come the ankles. After the first one Bernie'll ask, "How's it feel." "Lousy," I tell him. "You know it's lousy. It's too loose. When the hell are you going to learn? Hell, we might as well go over to the Vikings' dressing room. They wouldn't do any more harm than you're doing." But it's all right, and when he gets through with the ankles I stand on the table and he does the knees, a big job on the one with the scar and a little job on the good one.

I should have showed my scar to Spot Moore before I got it taped. He's been worried that maybe he has to have an operation to have some cartilage removed. "It's always better to go right away," I tell him. "Why don't you go in Monday and Fox'll fix you up. Seeing that it's only a cartilage it won't be too bad. Then when you get back to Arkansas you'll be the big razorback on campus." Some guys just have no sense of humor.

Doug, at least, understands me. We were sitting in front of our lockers after getting taped and he looked at himself and then at me and said, "Isn't this great sport?" and he started to laugh.

I looked down at my right leg taped from hip to foot and then at my left leg, foot, and knee all taped and I started laughing.

"Yeah, what the hell are you laughing at?" I said to him. "My right leg is all screwed up and my left leg is trying to get there."

"We'll have arthritis by the time we're thirty-five, forty at the latest," he said. "Who needs this crap? What the hell are we doing here anyway? Why don't we get dressed and go home?"

Just talking is a good distraction because this is the dead time in the locker room. Every time you look at the clock it seems earlier. The guys look for all kinds of ways to make the time pass. We all have a game program in our lockers when we arrive and a lot of the guys sit in front of their lockers and read. Some really try and get away from everything. They turn and put their heads into the locker itself and do their reading and thinking in there.

I thumb through the program every week. This week I'm looking for Tinglehoff. I find his picture and stare at his eyes to put the whammy on him, and I wonder if he's doing the same thing to me in their locker room on the other side of the field.

If I can I like to get a little bull session going with Doug and Bru, and maybe O'Bradovich will come over. Ed is always the last one in the locker room. He rushes in with his head down, throwing his clothes off as he goes, and hollering for Martell to tape him.

He's never had anybody but Martell tape him in all the years he's been with the Bears, and O'B is the only one Martell will tape. I guess O'B got started with Martell when he first joined the Bears and now he's grown a little superstitious and Martell obliges him.

All the little idiosyncrasies and peculiarities come out now. Seals always has Fox tape his hands. George has very small hands for a big man and with all that tape on them I wonder how he can ever pick up a ball. But he does. He picked up a fumble in Atlanta a couple of years ago and almost got it in for

137

a touchdown, and this year against New Orleans he beat me to a fumble in the end zone and got himself a touchdown.

Farmer has no expression. He shows no emotion at all. He's different, that's for sure. He reads poetry—Yeats, I read somewhere. Isn't he the one who wrote in one of his poems, "Things fall apart; the center will not hold?" Must have been a Bears fan.

Some of the guys spend all their time walking back and forth from locker to toilet. Dick Evey used to just stretch himself out on the floor and relax. Back in my Shakespeare reading days I used to treat the boys to a few choice renditions.

We were thinking of making a record and rewrote about forty of the famous Shakespearean speeches to put them in context—"Alas, poor Nitschke instead of poor Yorick; Yon Unitas has a lean and hungry look. Such men are dangerous." I'd usually give them a little "Once more unto the breach dear Bears!"

Sayers sits with his elbows on his knees and his chin in his thumbs. Percival does crossword puzzles. Cadile paces back and forth chewing his gum so hard I swear he's going to bite right through his own jawbone.

Shinnick always showers and shaves before the game. He wraps a towel around his waist and hums a tune to himself. Then he gets dressed and lights up a cigar and walks around the locker room from guy to guy. It's as if he were saying, "Okay, my work is done for the week. It's up to you guys now."

Bru painted our shoes, his and Doug's and mine. He painted them orange, but he did such a lousy job we chickened out and wouldn't wear them.

Little by little the clock moves and finally Mac puts down his crossword puzzle and says, "Let's go." That's a relief, and a release for all that nervous energy that's started to build up. I draw closer and closer to reality. And all through the warm-ups Abe is always somewhere around me growling, "Keep 'em up. Keep 'em going."

Then it's back to the locker room and the ritual of armoring ourselves. Some guys get dry. Some spit a lot. All the little adjustments of tape and strings and laces take on a super importance.

There are large blackboards at opposite ends of the locker

room. The defensive team forms a semicircle around Gibron and Shinnick in front of one while the offensive team gathers around head coach Jim Dooley in front of the other. The coaches review for the last time the plans for the day's game.

We've been going over this stuff for so long I dream about it. Yet everyone sits there like they've never heard it before. Buffone and O'B both look as though they're trying to absorb the blackboard right into their minds. Just so you don't have to think. You concentrate on not thinking.

Abe is talking about the runs and draws and how we have to contain Lee on his rollouts and zipouts and reviews their tendencies for the one-thousandth time this week. I look right at Abe, but his words sail right through me. It's not that I didn't hear him. Abe is not hard to hear.

Shinnick takes over and talks about the pass coverage and the red dogs and blitzes and who they like to throw to. He says we ought to go to the red dogs and blitzes early.

This is it. Let's go. It's coming on. Make 'em remember.

An official sticks his head in the door and yells, "five minutes coach!", and some of the guys really start getting nervous and fidgety. You go really dry and you think everybody in the room can hear you swallow. Some guys actually get the shakes and others start bouncing up and down.

There's no way they should beat us. No way. Worked hard all year . . . a finish you can be proud of. Play hard . . . do all I can. I won't be blocked. A rock . . . a wall . . . it's coming on . . . the doors open . . . the roar of the crowd. I'm on the field . . . I'm running . . . I feel fast . . . I feel light . . . I feel good. I feel great.

We're receiving. I lined up in the four-man blocking wedge on the twenty, along with George Seals, Randy Jackson, and Glen Holloway. We're going to return the kick to the side their kicker, Fred Cox, lines up on. He put the tee down on the right hash mark so we had an automatic return right. My man was the fifth man in, so I started counting and it was Kassulke, their strong safety, Karl Kassulke. And all week Abe has been harping about how Kassulke's the top man on their specialty teams.

139

I'll get him. I'll knock him right on his ass. Here we go. Here we go. It's a squib. It's short. Wait, wait wait . . .

I turned sideways to watch Cecil Turner. I have to watch him to keep the wedge together. Ok. Now. Back-back-back-right-right-right. Go! Go!

C'mon get him. There. He's hiding behind thirty-six.

The kickoff, any kickoff, seems like the most disorganized play in football. It isn't. Each man, whether on the kicking team or the receiving team has a specific assignment. Often it's a game of hide-and-seek in what looks like utter chaos. On the Bears receiving team the number-one man in the wedge takes out the first man down. The two and three men take out the second man. The guards up front peel back and take out the third and fourth men. I get the fifth man and that, theoretically, opens the alley for the return man to break through.

Goddamnit, where's he at? There, damn. He didn't make the damn tackle. At least he didn't get it.

But when I'm coming off the field there's Abe hollering, "Goddamnit Kassulke! Who's got him? Who's got Kassulke?"

"I got him. I got him. He didn't make the play."

There was a spot next to Jerry Moore and I dropped into it and asked him, "Kassulke didn't get in on it did he? When I looked he was just going over the pile."

Moore said, "No, Cecil was already tackled when he got there. That number thirty-six, that linebacker, he made the play."

Nix was starting at quarterback for us, but one run and two incomplete passes and I'm standing next to Abe ready to go in. "Anything special?"

"No, just go ahead with the game plan."

Huddle up, huddle up. Here we go. All right. Fifty-six crash—fifty-six crash to an odd crash post. *Remember to call it fast for George and the guys—it's Lee, Clint Jones, and Osborn.*

Red right, red right, Switch! Switch! *It's a trap. Get in there. Ummph. The guard the guard, get him. He's sliding. Bru . . . OK. Damn that Osborn and that guard. Right at my knee, trying to work it over to intimidate me right off. Trying to get me to protect myself instead of going to the ball.*

All right, all right, second and five—forty-six to an odd post fifty-four—forty-six to an odd post fifty-four.

*Green right—Now! C'mon move move Staley Staley. Here it is
. . . a Bob . . . the fullback going . . . stack 'em . . . ummph . . .
Good play, good play.*

Huddle up, huddle up. All right, third and three. Here we go.
Red right, red right. Osborn's cheated. Charley! Charley! Slant
them right . . . jam it . . . jam it. You son of a bitch. Get him, get
him. Don't let him score. That son of a bitch, he tackled me.
Don't let 'em get a cheap one. The tackle grabbed my foot, the
other guy had my arm. We were in a perfect defense. We had
it stacked up and would have stopped them cold. Jones bounces
off and goes for over forty yards. I hate to have them score on a
play like that—that goddamn holding.

All right, all right. Huddle up, huddle up. Let's keep it together. Those lucky bastards. Forty-six to an odd post—forty-six
to an odd post. Let's keep it together, let's hold them to a field
goal.

Red Left, red left. Sprint out! Sprint! *Back back . . . damn
damn. The flag went down. He calls that a touchdown?* Hey,
that's no touchdown. *On the one, just a quick flag pattern to
Grim.* He hit the flag, but at least they didn't call it a damn
touchdown.

All right, all right. Let's hold them here, let's hold them here.
I come up into the line in a three-point stance over Tinglehoff.
They always sneak for a yard or less. I had to get under Tinglehoff and straighten him up to drive him back and jam up the
middle.

Way to go, way to go. Second down, second down. Same
thing, same thing. *At practice we always fool around playing.
I'd play rushman or some other position. I always tell everybody
when I get too old to play linebacker I can always come up front
and be a rushman. Kind of anxious to see how it felt. It gave me
a taste. Just submarine in there, get under Tinglehoff. It felt
funny. Don't know where the ball is. Always looked for the ball,
but now just block the gap. Don't even know who has it. Don't
know if I could . . . always be looking for the ball.*

This time I yelled—Hut! Hut!—and snapped my head back
trying to draw them offside. Ed must have seen me move. He
started to go, and then the long count got to be too much for

Seals and he jumped. They got it in, but they were called for pushing Lee so we had to do it all over again.

All right, listen, stop them here. Hold them to a field goal. *They're not dumb enough to try another sneak.* Goal line sixty-one, goal line sixty-one. I'm in my normal position so I can see their formation. Green right! Green right! Hand-off to Osborn. A quick hand-off. They called it a touchdown, but it was questionable. He must have got one bar on his face mask to the goal line and they give it to him.

On the extra point I either try and slip by the center and clear a path to the kicker or drive straight into him. I drove straight into him, but I slipped and fell to my knees. I thought I'd jag him a little.

"All right, let's not start that holding crap again, Tinglehoff." He started to laugh while I started back upfield for the coming kickoff.

I came off and sat down next to Bru and started to say something to him when someone taps me on the shoulder. It's an usher, and he says, "Dick, can I get you to sign this?"

"Don't bother me now, for chrissake." Bru started to laugh and all of a sudden some kid jumps down and sits between us. "Hey kid, get out of here. You can't be sitting here."

The kid gets up and there's this same usher standing there with a camera and he said, "All right Johnny, that was good enough." I looked at Bru and said, "Can you believe this?" He was laughing like hell.

The offense worked it to third and two on our twenty-eight, but then Lonnie Warwick got Joe Moore for a yard loss. I got up and went to the sidelines to talk to Abe while Doug went out to block for Bobby Joe Green. His punt was no bargain. Bryant called for a fair catch just on the Vikings' side of the fifty. He juggled it and Gary Lyle got a little anxious and belted him. The flag went down. They moved it up to just over our forty.

"What do you want to do Abe, start going with the dogs?"

"Yeah, but not right away. Let 'em run a few plays first."

For chrissake they can kick a field goal from where they're at right now. We just started. We're in the hole already.

All right, all right, let's go. We have to stop them right here. Fifty-four post—fifty-four post. Eye left, eye left.

142

The second back . . . Jones . . . get over . . . fumble fumble . . . get it get it. Thought that guard was going to try. Let Yary sneak around and get me. Gave him a perfect angle. Good play Smitty. They said it was after the whistle. We needed that. Give us a good shot.

Okay, okay, huddle up, huddle up. Second and seven now. Let's hold 'em. Fifty-four to a post—fifty-four to a post. The Vikings come over the ball and I look over that line of purple helmets into their backfield. Green right—green right. A quick flare pass to Osborn. He breaks a tackle.

Get 'em get 'em . . . damn it . . . get him. We finally drag him down at the fourteen but they throw a flag on Charley Ford for grabbing his face mask. Now they have a first down on the seven.

Nothing to hold back for now. Might as well turn it loose. Maybe it'll get us going.

We're letting down, we're letting down. Let's keep it together. Let's go get them. Sixty-one burn—sixty-one burn. Both outside linebackers are going on a dog. They run a sweep to the right, toward Doug. He's in their backfield before the play even gets going. Osborn tried to bow even deeper to get around but Doug nailed him.

Good play Doug. Way to go. Good play. All right second and fifteen, second and fifteen. Same thing, same thing. Sixty-one burn—sixty-one burn. Red left! Red left!

Got the first back. Lousy fake. Watch him . . . watch him . . . go . . . pass . . . get him . . . ummph.

I saw Osborn fake a lousy block and slide off. I knew it was the screen. My mind just went blank and I took off. I didn't think of anything till I got there. Some lineman tried to cut me off but I just brushed by him. And then just before I hit him I started thinking, should I try and strip him of the ball, or should I just make sure I tackle him. I just made sure. Now we had them back to the twenty-two.

All right, all right. They have to go for the score. Let's not give it away, play it smart. Fifty-four post—fifty-four post. Red left! Red Left!

You've got to figure they've got the field goal. Just don't give them more.

143

Draw! Draw! *Don't press the issue. Just make the stop.* Anyway I can. It might not be pretty, but we stop him. They tried to double-team me again, but Yary wasted too much time fooling around with Willie.

So Cox comes in and kicks a field goal and now we're ten points down.

I give my old pal Tinglehoff a good shot and then the return team is on the field again. Cecil says Abe wants a return left. That gives me the number-one man, Bob Bryant.

Cox gave it a good boot. Cecil takes it about a yard deep and we start to go. I look for Bryant and go after him. But I never do catch him. He just keeps backing up, backing up until I'm chasing him out of bounds.

Time for a drink. Take the helmet off, sit down on the bench, and let just a little bit of water run down your throat so's you can feel it going right through the pipes all the way down to your stomach. That feels good.

Third and ten on our own thirty-six and it's time to get up and get ready to go to work again. Nix hits George Farmer for sixteen yards and a first down so I get down on one knee along the sidelines to watch. But there's no more to see. Three plays later we have to punt again. This time Bobby Joe kicks it out of bounds on the Vikings' twenty-one.

All right, all right. Let's stop them down here. Keep them bottled up, take it way from them. Fifty-four to a post—fifty-four to a post. Let's go. Red right tight—tight red right. Willie Holman beats his man clean and gets Osborn for a two-yard loss. Good job Willie, great play.

All right, second and twelve. Fifty-six crash—fifty-six crash. That puts both Bru and me behind our defensive tackles. Give Lee something new to look at. Straight hand-off to Jones. *Goddamnit, I was late. Son of a . . .*

Huddle up, huddle up. All right, third and four, third and four. Put the pressure on him. Forty-six tight post to a sixty-one burn—forty-six tight post to a sixty-one burn. Blow in there now. Break—red left, red left. *Back back back . . . get him get him. Couldn't get it. Good. They have to kick it.*

It's me and Tinglehoff again. I tried to slip by him to make him come after me on one side to open up an aisle to let Smitty go up the middle. If we get good enough pressure from the outside he has got to commit himself one way or the other and give someone a shot at the punter. But they got it away.

Nix sneaked for a first down, our second of the game, on the forty-two. I appreciated the rest. Then he hit Bob Wallace for thirteen. Charley West was called for interfering with Farmer at the thirty-two. They made another first down, and then got it down to the fourteen. We've had so little to cheer about lately that we started to get excited along the sidelines. If we could put one in now we'd really make a ball game out of it and wake everybody up.

On third and three West stepped in front of Farmer who was running a little square out and took off down the sideline. *Damnit Damnit* . . . get him . . . get him. He's gone. Goddamnit, he's got a clear shot.

All of a sudden Joe Moore started running like hell from clear across the field. I never thought he could catch him. But he closed that gap and slowed West up. Page was running with West and he tried to take Moore out. But somehow Moore faked him and got around him and made the tackle. That was a helluva play. It made me feel a lot better just to know we weren't giving up. I thought to myself, this guy really showed something. Page had position on him, but he never gave up. He ran him down. Could just as easily have dogged it, given up on it. Who would have known the difference? But they had the ball on our six-yard line, and we still had to face up to that.

Come on, let's go now. We have to stop them here. No touchdown—they get no touchdown. Six-one goal line—Six-one goal line. Get tough now. Get tough. Break. Red left! Red Left! *To the left* . . . *To the left.* They tried to run a slant left but Doug turned it in and we were all there to stop him. I tried to take the ball away from him but couldn't quite manage it.

Way to go, way to go. Second and four. Only a yard, get tough. Same thing. Six-one goal line—six-one goal line. Green right! Green right! *The fullback* . . . *the fullback. Stop him* . . . *jam* . . . No gain, no gain. Way to go, way to go.

All right, all right. This is it, this is it. Third and four—stop them here and we're still in it, we'll still be in it. Make them settle for a field goal. Six-one goal line with a wide burn—six-one goal line with a wide burn. They have to pass now, and Joe Taylor is going to blitz from his cornerback spot. Tight green left! Tight green left! *Sprint . . . sprint . . . get him . . . Joe . . . Joe . . . great play Joe . . . aw shit . . . goddamnit.*

Joe nailed Lee back on the twelve. Seals was coming in hard. He tried to jump over the pile at the last minute and tripped. They dropped the flag on Seals for hitting him after the whistle. He was trying to miss him, and even then the official was late dropping the flag. As if he was trying to make up his mind. That's chickenshit.

It's getting real bad with officials. They seem to be losing control of the game. When we look at the films we see a lot of teams getting screwed on bad calls. Of course we always think we get the worst of it. Maybe we all do, but it seems that we're always getting them on key plays. Willie got clipped in the Rams game and they got a touchdown on the play. Holloway in the Denver game. It was a draw play. It looked like the official saw the play was going to go and he threw the flag. He had his hand in his pocket. He was reaching for the flag before anything happened. When Douglass was in the end zone he threw it down and called Holloway for holding.

Somehow it seems that we get it worse than the other guys. I don't know, maybe it's just that the coaches make it seem that way. But sometimes you can actually see an official with his hand in his pocket when it looks like something good is going to happen for us.

"Hey, stick it," I told that guy. I always yell and bitch at them. I'm more or less jagging them, making mountains out of sand castles. If it's at all close I'm yelling. I think they're catching on to me because if it is close and I yell they say, "C'mon you know it Dick." And I'll say, "Listen, call 'em right will you." You can't ever admit that they're right. But here we make a helluva stand and then they throw a flag on a chickenshit thing like that.

All right, all right, we've got to do it all over again. We can do it. Let's go. Forty-six crash—forty-six crash. *Watch the quick pass. Watch the quickie.*

Red left! Red left! Reed! Reed! All right, good Play Willie!

They tried a sweep to their left but Willie came around and made the tackle.

Let's go, let's go. Second and six now, let's hold them. *They got to throw now . . . they got to throw.* Forty-six post—forty-six post. *Look in the huddle. Catch the count. He said on two . . . on two.* It's on two! It's on two! Green Left! Green left! *Drop . . . drop . . . back . . . goddamnit. We should have blitzed him again, but they were expecting it.*

Just like that play in Baltimore last year—Unitas to Roy Jefferson. We had them 17–0 then lost 21–20. Jefferson ran to the middle and then cut to the far corner to beat Bennie McRae. It was the identical play, only the people changed—Lee to Bob Grim.

Back to Tinglehoff again. We wacked each other and then Seals fell over me and I turned and said, "You son of a bitch." I didn't know it was him, and he turned and then said, "Oh, oh, it's you."

Tinglehoff looked at both of us as if to say, well, we've got them arguing now. We've got them fighting each other. So there we were, 17–0 and the second quarter isn't even five minutes old. And we gave it all to them—Jones ran on a busted play; the penalty on Lyle; and the cheap penalty on Seals.

We had a right return on. Cox kicked a low sailer, like a knuckle ball. I started back to get it, but Cecil came up in time and got it and ran it out over the thirty. I didn't even go to the bench. I just knelt on the sideline and took another drink. We had it third and five, but only made four. Then Bobby Joe hit one about sixty yards into their end zone.

All right. Let's go let's go let's go let's go. Let's take it away from them. Let's turn it around. Fifty-six crash buckeye—fifty-six crash buckeye. That's a one-man red dog. Doug's going. Green right! Green right. *The fullback—A perfect play—ran right into Doug. Lost a yard.* Way to go Doug.

Second and eleven. Second and eleven. Forty-six post and this time I'm going—forty-six post. *Catch the count . . . catch the count . . . I got it.* I thought I had it. My mind went blank. Lee yelled something. I shot the gap between guard and center. I made a complete sweep of their backfield. Then something told me don't hit anybody, you can still get back outside. I ran completely around the backs and everybody started standing up looking at me and I went swooping around O'B and Bru and back to my position.

Bru was laughing like hell and Doug came over and whispered, "Hey Dick, I think you were offside on that one." So they gave me five and I couldn't even bitch about it.

Everybody was snickering in the huddle. So I said to myself, just call it fast and get the hell out of there or else you'll never stop laughing. Fifty-six crash—fifty-six crash. Let's go. Green right! Green right! They ran the Bob play to the weak side and someone missed him and they made a first down.

Fifty-six crash—fifty-six crash. All right, let's go. Red right! Red right! *The halfback . . . your man . . . your key . . . get over . . . that's it . . . ummph.* It's a beautiful game when things work out that way. There I was and there was Jones.

All right, let's go. Second and ten. Here we go. Fifty-six crash to a Sticky Sam. Doug, Bru, Smitty—we're all going. Let's get a good jump now. Okay, break. Green right! Green right! *Go go go . . . get him . . . Smitty's got him. The ball . . . the ball . . . get the damn thing.* Lee fumbled and the ball was bouncing around loose. It went right by Doug, and Willie Holman was trying to grab it along the sideline. The officials said we never had possession. I start hollering that it should be our ball.

Those bastards. Come on, let's get it this time. Okay, let's mix it up. Third and fourteen. Let's show them a little Jill-dog. Go get 'em Spot. Red right! Red right! Jerry Moore goes flying in on a safety blitz and dumps Jones before he can get started.

Then it's me and Tinglehoff again on our little game and I go over and kneel on the sideline. I don't usually spend so much time there, but this is the last game and I want to watch Page and Eller in action. But it's not for long. Nix's third-down pass is tipped by Eller and it falls incomplete. Bobby Joe hits it good again and it goes about fifty yards into the end zone.

Three plays, a punt, and we're out there again. These guys are going to get tired of looking at us.

Huddle up, huddle up. All Right. Fifty-four—fifty-four. Red left! Red left! Pass! Pass! *Not much you can do about that. Not when they run it like that.* Lee just dropped straight back and hit Gene Washington on a quick square out. That's seven yards.

All right, let's go. Second and three. Fifty-four—fifty-four. Red left! Red left! Fake a dog . . . fake a . . . *Reed Reed . . . right right . . . get over . . . get . . . ummph . . . Not soon enough.*

All right, let's dig in a little now. Let's take it away. Fifty-four—fifty-four. Watch the rollout. Break! Red left! Red left! Roll! Roll! *Get him get him . . . Willie Willie . . . the ball . . . get the ball . . . get the . . . damn Tinglehoff.*

Way to go, way to go. Keep it going. We'll get a break. It can't always bounce back to them. All right. What is it? Second and twenty-two. Probably a pass. Forty-six with the tackles crossing. Watch the screens and draws. Let's go. Red left! Red left! Sweep! Sweep! *Get over . . . get over . . . turn him . . . all right.*

We got them now. Third and what is it? Almost twenty. Forty-six post—forty-six post. Just stay awake. Break! Roll! Roll! *Go with flow. Stay with him. End coming across . . . take . . . oh . . . what the hell.* Washington saw he had Charlie Ford beat. It was supposed to be a sideline, but he just kept going deep, waving his hand to Lee. We have them third and about eighteen and they break it for fifty yards.

Give them another score now and we might as well go home. C'mon, let's get tough. Better make a forty-six with a burn—forty-six burn. C'mon, break! Eye! Eye! *The second man . . . the second man.* Sweep! Sweep! *Get over get over . . . turn him . . . now . . . get rid of . . . hey . . . goddamn clip . . . flag.*

I started to say something to their guard, Ed White, but I saw the flag. He tried to cut me off on the sweep, but I had control of him with my hands. I was just waiting for the runner to make his move, inside or outside. I slowed up because I'd have a better shot if he went wide. I started to throw White away from me and as he was sort of sliding behind he threw and clipped me. One of the officials saw it.

Lee came over and said, "What'd he do, clip you?" Maybe he was trying to make friends with some small talk. "Yeah," I said, "I guess he did." Hell, all I was thinking was that it was about time we caught a break. That moved them back past our forty.

All right, maybe it'll turn around. Let's really give them something good. Forty-six Isaacs Double Baker burn—forty-six Isaacs

Double Baker burn. Red right! Red right! Pass! Pass! *Back Back ... get to hash mark ... drop it you bast ... good ... hey ... who's it on?*

Them. We'll take it. Offensive interference. That's loss of down too. Good. Okay, okay. Let's go. Now they've got like third and forty. Same thing, forty-six Isaacs Double Baker burn—forty-six Isaacs Double Baker burn. Break! Red left! Red left! *Get him get that ... oh my god ... what the hell is going on? We give it right back.*

Interference. They call interference on Smitty. That puts us right back where we were about six plays ago. What the hell you gonna do? I wasn't in any hurry to get down there to our huddle. I was taking my time and the Vikings were already starting to the huddle up. So I thought I'd stop and listen in.

"C'mon in," White invited. And then Tinglehoff said, "Yeah Dick, c'mon in." And I said, "Hell, it wouldn't help us. Even if we knew the play it wouldn't help us."

I didn't even want to go into our huddle. "Doug, Willie, what the hell is going on? What should we do? You think we ought to change some of these defenses to give those guys some help back there?" They both just shrugged.

The Vikings did us a favor and ran the ball the next play and then Joe Taylor made a good play on John Henderson. That brought us to third down again. We ran the "double Baker burn" at them again and Lee missed Reed on the swing pass. I started bitching at the official that Jones was blocking me before the ball was thrown. He wouldn't buy it. Just trying to give them a tougher field goal, that's all. But Cox missed this one anyway.

About three or four of us were coming off the field together and Abe was standing there on the sidelines bitching and hollering, "What the hell's going on out there. How come those guys are so damn wide open?" I didn't have the answer. I just wanted to take a blow.

Three plays, a punt, and we were back in. Bryant made a good run back to put it in our territory just over the fifty.

I called a "fifty-six" and they were in a red left. Lee dropped straight back and hit Bill Brown deep again. He got behind Smitty. He caught the ball, went down, and then got up and started to run again. They finally got him down on the two. I started bitching at the ref again. "Hell, Smitty made enough contact that he should have been called down on about the fifteen."

They did us a favor by running the ball again. Lee kept it on a roll right. Ford came up and hit him hard. The ball popped out and Tony McGee fell on it for us on the three. With about thirty seconds left I figured even our offense could kill the clock now. They did, and we headed into the locker room.

It was quiet in there. It doesn't have the old sounds anymore. There used to be something musical about the click-click-clickety-click of all those cleats on the concrete. But now we wear those rubber Astroturf shoes and walk on carpets. And when you're a dead-ass team you'd think you were at a wake.

We figured this is it. We figured that Moore might have come close to an interception once and he did make a couple of tackles, and with them leading 17–0 they sure weren't going to be throwing it around. So I got the bottle and the rest of the guys passed around the paper cups and I broke open the Mumms. We raised our paper cups in salute to Moore and had about a drop apiece. For chrissake don't tell the Old Man.

So we sat there, the defensive team, looking at each other and shaking our heads, with a bunch of crumpled paper water cups all over the floor. George started to say something like, "I don't know where I'll be next year, but I'll miss you guys." Abe stuck his head in and called us out for a meeting. The offense was in the room across the way.

"Their frequencies are the same as they always are," Abe said. "Run, run, pass on third down. There's nothing we have to change. We're playing all right. Just keep it up, that's all."

But it wasn't the best of Abe. He could see, just as we could, that there was no way our offense was going to get eighteen points. He tried to make it sound as enthusiastic as he could, but it wasn't the best of Abe. If the game were closer he would have been hollering and bitching and chewing plenty of ass the way those receivers were getting open deep. They could run that anytime they wanted to, it seemed.

"Anybody have anything to say?" Abe asked. "No? Okay, when you're ready let's go across the hall." We joined our offensive brethren and they were just sitting around waiting for Dooley to say something.

He started to talk, talking real fast, about some offensive changes. Douglass was going in at quarterback. Then he started saying something like, "Hang tough defense. Just hang in there. We'll get something going for you."

I couldn't force myself to listen. He was talking fast, like he always does, and it was just going right past me. It was just a blank. Some of the other guys started to say something, started to talk it up, but that had no effect either.

Another feeling, I never thought I'd ever have a feeling like this going into a game, a league game. Sure, maybe in the Pro Bowl. You can understand that, but even then you shouldn't. As we're going out I said to myself, "Well, there's just one more half." *This is it. Just this and it's all over. Make it something to remember, not something to forget. Give them something to remember.* And it worked. When I came out of the ramp and hit the field I really felt like playing.

We kicked off and they put it in play on their twenty. The first play Lee drops straight back and hits Jones down the sideline for over fifteen yards.

Come on. Let's wake up now, let's get going. Vacation's over. Fifty-four crash—fifty-four crash. Break! Green left! Green left!

The hand-off goes to Jones. Tony McGee breaks through his block and smears the play before they can get started. Good play Tony. Way to go.

In the huddle I call a blitz. Jerry Moore is going on a safety blitz. It looks good at the line, but Doug calls, "Can it! Can it!" That takes it off. They're in a red left and they run a sweep to our left. Jones breaks it for over twenty yards. If I would have run the blitz the way I wanted to we would have just stacked it up. It was the perfect defense for that call. That's what you get for letting people talk you out of things.

Come on, come on. Let's go. Fifty-six crash buckeye—fifty-six crash buckeye. *This time you're not changing it.* Green right! Green Right! Pass! Pass! Just the same as the first half, the tight end is running free and clear again, but this time Lee overthrows him.

Now I start having doubts about the wisdom of that buckeye. If I put Doug over the tight end instead of red dogging he can

152

jam him on the line so that he'll have trouble getting deep. Doug left it up to me.

We managed to tighten up a little and Lee threw two incompletions on second and third down. He made up for it though with his punt. It went dead on our one. I just stood there looking at that damn ball just lying there near the goal line. *What the hell. What the hell you going to do? These guys really have it going for them.*

I just walked over to Abe and shrugged and Bobby Douglass ran out on the field and got booed. Everybody just booed the hell out of him. I figured I might as well stay there. I'd be going in soon anyway.

After two tries on the ground we had it third and seven on the four. I was going to give Doug a blow and block for Bobby Joe's punt, which I figured would be coming up if the Vikings didn't get a safety. It looked like they had Douglass trapped about five yards deep in the end zone, but he got away and it didn't even look like he threw it hard, like he just wanted to sail it so Farmer could run under it. That ball just went and went and sailed and sailed and Farmer made a helluva diving catch and the play covered sixty-five yards from scrimmage, and Douglass must have thrown the damn ball about seventy-five yards.

Everyone who was booing him when he ran on the field three plays ago was now cheering like hell. It looked like a good time to get a rest. They got it down to the five or six for a first down, but Gordon and West were mixing it up and they threw the flag on Gordon.

"Listen Abe, why don't we fake the field goal and have Douglass throw a pass? What the hell have we got to lose? What the hell good are three points?" Abe was willing to buy it, but Dooley said no. He wanted to get on the board. So halfway through the third quarter we make it 17–3.

They were caught clipping on the kickoff and we have them pinned back inside their ten. *What the hell. We've done it before. You never know. Let's get them.*

Okay, okay. Let's stop 'em right here. Give 'em nothing. Play it tough. Fifty-four crash—fifty-four crash. Let's go. Break! Red left! Red left! Jones Jones! *Get that son . . . ummph.*

All right, all right. We gave him too much. Let's get it up. Fifty-six crash—fifty-six crash. Play it tough. Break! Eye right! Eye right! *Pitch . . . pitch . . . get the . . . ummph.*

Way to go, way to go Bru. Third and six, third and six. Let's keep them here. Okay, forty-six post—forty-six post. Break! Red left! Red left! Rollout! Rollout! *Back back. Get in the flow. Get it . . . knock it . . . goddamnit . . . son of a bitch. That same goddamn play all day. Son of a . . .*

I just turned around and stood there looking, wondering what the hell was happening back there. What the hell is going on? Every time they need some yardage they hit that same pass, to the tight end or a back, running a post. Somebody's got to be asleep. So instead of us getting the ball around midfield on a punt they've got a first down around our forty. It makes you want to puke.

They tried the same thing again. Why not? It works just about every time. But this time Charley Ford came across the field and broke it up on a helluva play. But he didn't get up. He just lay there, and his face was all bloody. He must have caught Bill Brown's face mask when they both went up.

The doctor and trainer were out on the field and I started to stroll over toward the sideline where Abe was standing. Time was out, but one official came over to me and said, "If you go over there and talk to him I'll have to give you a penalty." I started to turn back toward the middle of the field and I could hear Abe hollering, "Come here! Come here!"

I turned and hollered back, "I can't talk to you, because if I do I'm going to get a penalty." And the official came over and said, "No, you can talk to him, but if you do I'm going to give you a penalty." While this one guy is splitting verbal hairs another one runs over and all excited says, "You can't talk to him. If you do you'll get a penalty." "Hey, I wasn't anyway, so what's the big deal?"

We stopped Osborn for no gain on the following play, but then on the next one Lee hit Grim on a short post and we missed a couple of tackles on him and he ran all the way. All I can do is stand there swearing. But after a while even that gets kind of old.

On the kickoff I went after Bryant again and the damn guy

ran out of bounds, so I threw at him anyway just as he was going out. Three plays and we punted and I went out to block for Bobby Joe again.

We ran a blitz and Smith got Jim Lindsey for a five-yard loss on a sweep. A pass to Henderson was incomplete. They try another sweep with Lindsey and he's hit, fumbles, and Holmes recovers for us inside the Vikings' thirty.

If we hadn't given so much away . . . all those cheap points . . . We gave them. If we went for the score . . . still haven't got this one in yet. No sense figuring anything, but this coulduv been a game. We just beat ourselves. You always do.

Douglass threw to Farmer for a first down on the six, threw three straight incompletions and then on fourth down threw to Gordon for the touchdown. I went back into block for the extra point and that made it 24–10. We're sneaking up on them. But you never know.

We stopped them on three plays and on the first play of the fourth quarter they punted. Two plays later Joe Moore got the ball popped out of his arm and Wally Hilgenberg recovered for them.

Standing on the sidelines watching, O'B comes over and says, "Well, this is probably the last time. I don't think I'll be back next year." He was racked up pretty bad, but he played anyway and now Abe's sending him in and then he'll take him out so he can come off by himself and get an ovation, it being his day and all.

They get called for offensive interference on the first play, which sets them back inside their forty-five. Lee completes a couple, but it's not enough for a first down, just enough to get Cox in position for a field goal. He kicks one damn near fifty yards, and if we did have any chance at all that just about finished it. Now we'd need three touchdowns to beat them.

Douglass started to move them, or maybe the Vikings figured they'd just give up the short gains. But whatever they were thinking didn't matter because Bryant intercepted one and ran it back to midfield.

Norm Snead came in at quarterback and I figured they were just going to put the freeze on the ball with only about seven minutes remaining now. He ran the first one, and then threw an incompletion. He completed a swing pass to Brown, but we got to him before he could turn upfield.

They punted to Smith. Now the Gingerbread Man never, never calls for a fair catch. They can be stepping on his toes and standing on his shoulders, but he'll never call for the fair catch. He thinks if he can break past the first wave he stands a good chance of going all the way. But not this time. He was hit and fumbled and the Vikings recovered on our three.

The word is that you can get to Snead with the blitz because it gets him a little rattled. Not that I really blame him. So I figured we might as well be as aggressive as possible.

Come on, come on. Keep it together. Let's go after this guy. He doesn't like it. Let's go get him. Forty-six double burn with a Sticky Sam—forty-six double burn with a Sticky Sam. Let's go. Red right! Red right! *Go go go . . . get him . . . atta boy Joe . . . go . . . go . . . what the . . .*

Joe Taylor went busting through just as Snead was attempting to hand off to Lindsey. The ball rolled loose and Joe picked it up and started to run. He had a cinch touchdown. But they called it back. They claimed there was enough contact to consider Joe downed. Just the opposite call they gave us when Bill Brown got up and ran in the second quarter.

I went over to Bobby Joe and said, "Listen, if we go in there let's throw the ball instead of kicking it." Then I went and told Abe the same thing. "Why don't we put Gary Lyle in motion and snap the ball on a quick count and if he's open throw it to him. They're supposed to be such geniuses on those special teams. Let's see what they do with that." So Abe said, "Sure, go ahead. Let's see what happens." So we went in there and I guess Lyle didn't look soon enough or he wasn't open because Bobby Joe went ahead and kicked it.

They ran one up the middle and on the next play we put on a big blitz and Jimmy Gunn got to Snead and dumped him for a big loss. I called another big blitz in the huddle and when Snead came over the center he looked at me and he started to smile a little. He made a face as if to say, you guys are coming again, aren't you. You SOB's are coming. Jerry Moore was inching up and I nodded, yes, we're coming. We're going to get your ass. Here we come.

We came like hell, and he had to scramble and he had no where to dump the damn ball. He had to eat it. But he got out of bounds before we could really get to him.

Our offense held the ball for a few plays but they ran out of downs and the Vikings took over. At least I was going to finish the game on the field. Finish the season on the field. Doug was hurting, he got a few whacks in the knee during the year and along the sidelines he was saying how he just wanted to finish the season.

One more series. It's down to this. Less than a minute, then you have to wait a whole year. A few plays and it's all over. Go out with your head up.

All right, all right. Let's go. This is it, this is the last series. If he doesn't like the blitz let's give it to him anyway. Let's just go all out. I'm going to just shoot up the middle. Corners just go man-to-man. Everybody else, let's get them. They aren't going to throw the damn ball anyway.

Snead got the hand-off away just out of my reach. I was stumbling over some bodies and I turned and saw Doug go down. The other back got him on a crack-back. It's like getting blindsided. It went through my mind instantly. I knew he was hurt. I felt like I caused it by calling the red dog. Playing his position normally he wouldn't have been as vulnerable to that kind of block.

But I thought by calling the red dog no one would get hurt. The red dog would get everybody going instead of waiting for them to come to us, if we were laying back. But I felt real bad for him because he wanted to finish.

It all came tumbling through my mind. He was playing out his option. He almost signed and then changed his mind because he wanted to try and play with a winner. I didn't know what it was at first, so I unsnapped his chin strap. He was lying there saying, "I knew it. I knew it. I knew they were going to run that damn play. And I knew something would happen."

Fox and Bernie ran out and checked his knee. He said he couldn't feel anything. It went numb. "I'm going to stay in," he said. "There's only one more play." Fox said, "Like hell you are, we're going to carry you off this field."

"No, no, you're not," Doug said. "No stretcher. Let me walk

157

off. No help. I want to walk off on my own. If I can't finish I'm going to walk off." He got up and they watched him take a few steps. It looked like he could make it, so they let him walk off the field.

They had to run another play. Snead took it and just fell down with it. They went back into their huddle. They were just standing there. The referee was standing between us and I looked at him and made a T with my hands, the signal for a time-out.

He gave me a funny look, as if to say, c'mon, get serious, and shook his head from side to side. No.

Snead saw me and started laughing. Tinglehoff and the rest of them started looking at me and they stood there laughing and hollering at me as the seconds blinked off the electric clock.

The gun went off. Everybody started running. White came over, and Jim Marshall and I yelled to Tinglehoff. We all shook hands and said a few words and then they were gone, and suddenly I was alone in the middle of the field.

Let's not quit. Let's not end it. Let's keep going. C'mon Page . . . Eller . . . Mick . . . Krause . . . White . . . All you guys. Let's go, let's go.